$2.75

The Story of Saint Nicholas

BY MILDRED C. LUCKHARDT

Illustrated by Gordon Laite

Christmas is a time of giving. On the first Christmas, God gave his son to the world; and, we are told, wise men brought to the infant gifts of gold, frankincense, and myrrh. About three centuries later, in a part of the world we now call Turkey, a boy marveled at men who could give such fine gifts and not leave their names.

When that boy, Nicholas, grew older, he became a bishop of the Christian church, and he, too, gave gifts without telling who had given them. He gave mostly to children, but he is best known for the dowries he gave to three girls who had none and who could not marry without them.

After Nicholas died, he was called Saint Nicholas. Other people followed his example by giving gifts without telling, and legends grew up around the deeds that he was said to have done. At last some of these legends became the basis for the Santa Claus we know today.

(Continued on back flap)

ABINGDON PRESS

New York   Nashville

The Story of Saint Nicholas

by Mildred Luckhardt

illustrated by Gordon Laite

NEW YORK ABINGDON PRESS NASHVILLE

To Children Everywhere in the World
May they all share in the happiness
brought by gifts given as Saint Nicholas gave.

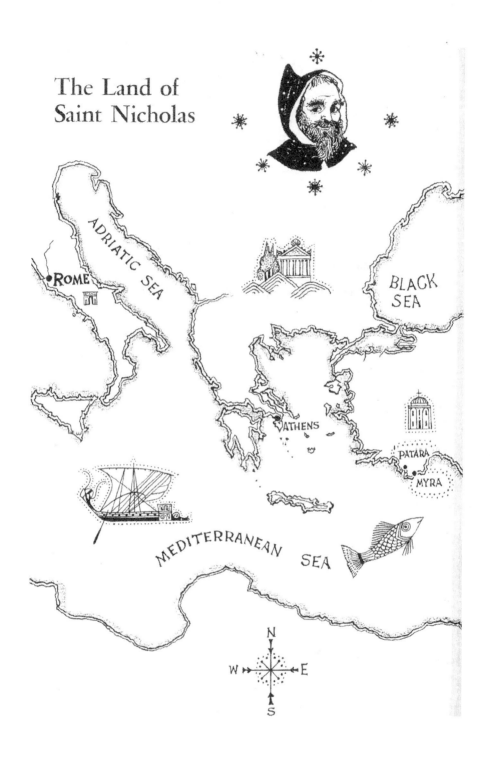

The Land of
Saint Nicholas

ADRIATIC SEA

ROME

BLACK SEA

ATHENS

PATARA

MYRA

MEDITERRANEAN SEA

N
W E
S

Contents

BOOK I

THE STORY OF SAINT NICHOLAS

1

The Wonderful World
of Saint Nicholas

NICHOLAS stood by the front door of his home and looked down at the shining blue waters of Patara Bay. Then he ran to the back of the house and looked eagerly up the steep mountain path. But there was no sign of his Uncle John. The work at the house of Thaddeus was taking a long time.

He scuffed impatiently as he walked once more to the front of the house. There he could see Thaddeus' silk ship anchored far out, near the harbor mouth. Nick was to take important papers to the ship when his uncle returned with them. The silk ship, like all of the ships in the harbor, was being made ready for the first spring sailing. Everyone in Patara was busy. Everyone but Nick; and he longed to be helping. He did not want to spend his school vacation standing still.

"Anya!" he called to his uncle's housekeeper. "What can be keeping Uncle John?"

Anya made no answer. So Nick called again. "Anya," he said, "if Uncle John is not on his way home, I am going to run to the wharves for a while. Maybe the spice warehouse is being unloaded today. If it is, I want to be there."

He tramped around the side of the house. Still no answer from Anya. But he could hear her broom thumping near the door as he looked again along the rocky path that curved sharply up the pine-covered mountain. High in a clearing, about a mile beyond, stood the sprawling weather-beaten house of Thaddeus. His family had once been rich and noble, and the people of Patara still looked upon him as a nobleman, although he now had little money. The big house had once been elegant; but now it was bare and shabby.

All the money that Thaddeus had, he had put into the cargo of the silk ship; and he had borrowed money from moneylenders besides. If the silk cargo brought a good price, Thaddeus could pay his debts and provide comfortably for his frail wife and their three little girls. But if the ship should be lost at sea, or captured by pirates, he would never recover his fortune.

As Nick stood thinking, he heard the far-off jingle of bells. A donkey train was coming down the mountain road.

Anya heard the sound, too, and ran outdoors, not stopping to throw down her broom. "Four donkey trains have passed within these last two days," she said, peering up the road.

The days before spring sailings always brought a number of donkey trains from lands beyond the mountains, laden with goods to be shipped from Patara. The usual donkey train passed through only twice a month, going to Patara and then eastward to the city of Myra.

8

Soon the little brown beasts, carrying bulging packs of richly woven rugs, rounded the bend. From habit, the lead donkey headed for Uncle John's well, and Anya and Nick hurried to draw water. Before the donkey could drink, however, the driver turned him away.

"Do not trouble to draw water," he said. "We are in haste. The animals drank at the nobleman's well."

Nicholas watched the donkeys go, wanting to run down the dusty road to the wharves with them. "Why do those papers have to go to the silk ship today?" he asked impatiently. "It is too early for ships to leave. Just as winter turns into spring there are often windstorms that can wreck a ship. And pirates will be waiting for the first to venture out. Surely Thaddeus' ship will not be sailing yet."

Anya's mouth closed grimly. "As soon as the papers are ready, the ship will sail," she answered. "Roman silk merchants pay high prices for the first shipload to reach them in the spring. They cannot be sure when more will arrive——with storms and pirates."

She went indoors and flailed her broom at a speck on a rafter. Nick followed to listen as she went on. "That raw silk came all the way from China to the looms on the island of Cos; then it came to Patara; and now it goes on to Rome. It is valuable, and our noble Thaddeus paid much for it. He must get much in return. The moneylenders will not wait long for payment."

Nicholas walked outside and looked long at the silk ship. He was glad he could help Thaddeus. But he did wish his Uncle John would hurry. He glanced around again, and beyond

9

the rooftops of Patara he could see the trade route from the east. A caravan was moving toward the city now, the camels swaying beneath the great loads they carried.

Loudly, Nick counted the beasts. He went on and on. "Thirty camels, thirty-one camels, thirty-two camels——"

Anya broke in. "Such a noisy boy you are. Lazy, too! Only lazy people have time to stand counting camels."

Nick stopped counting out loud. Instead he picked up his flute and counted the camels in groups of four on the flute. "Tootle-ootle-ootle-ootle. Tootle-ootle-ootle-ootle."

When he reached camel forty-eight, Anya cried out, "Nonsense! Only a thousand jackals could make the noise you do. Look at the fire. Do flute screechings keep the fire burning? Fires need wood. When your uncle returns he will be hungry."

Nicholas ran to the shed for wood, but his mind was still on the camels. In his haste, his head bumped a basket of walnuts

on a high shelf. Down went the walnuts. And down went Nicky, slipping and sliding on the rolling nuts. Another basket on the shelf tipped and walnuts pelted him like stinging rain. Then the basket toppled down on his head.

Fumbling, Nick pulled the basket off and began to laugh. Slipping on walnuts, rolling, crunching them underfoot, he gathered up an armful of wood and started for the house.

Uncle John was opening the front door when Nicholas carried the wood in. For the first time Nick noticed how tired and thin his uncle was. When he took off his worn brown cloak, his long, plain robe, belted at the waist, seemed too large for his tall, lean frame. The scar from a pirate's sword on his left cheek showed plainly, as it always did when he was tired. The work of a seaport pastor was hard, and Uncle John had been a pastor for a long time.

Nicholas laid the worn cloak on a bench while Uncle John smiled and warmed his hands by the fire. "The air is chill with a rising wind," he said. "I'm cold and hungry. That stew smells good, Anya. You are the best cook I ever heard of."

She hurried to get a bowl, complaining, "You work too hard. You do not remember to eat. We ate our midday meal some time ago. Why do you never take time for your own comfort?"

Uncle John explained, "You take such good care of us, Anya, that I need not waste time taking care of myself. Besides, you know it is always this way before the spring sailing. Everyone has letters to write, messages to send, chests to store. And this morning Thaddeus' papers took longer to prepare than we had planned."

Nicholas was impatient to be off with the papers, but Anya

11

talked at great length about Thaddeus' misfortunes. "If anything goes wrong with this silk ship, his lovely little girls will
be almost as poor as beggars," she wailed. Then she whirled
around, demanding sharply, "Nicholas, why do you stand idly?
You have a long, hard row to that ship."

Nick laughed. "I'll go as soon as I get the papers from
Uncle John, but he hasn't been able to give them to me."

Uncle John turned and took a roll of papers from his robe.
"Here you are. Run along with them now."

"Guard them well," Anya called as Nick left the house.

Nicholas waved in reply and ran downhill toward the wharf
where their small boat was tied. When he reached the rowboat, he noticed a sharp wind from the sea. Hoping it would
get no worse, he fastened the roll of papers securely in his
tunic and shoved off. He rowed with long, sure strokes as
straight as he could toward the distant silk ship. Already its
sails were being hoisted to catch the wind.

How rough the bay was growing! Waves rolled in from the
sea. As Nicholas pulled sturdily past a big Roman grain ship,
spray stung his eyes. He pulled on, past a Greek ship, and a
Spanish, and an Egyptian. Everywhere seamen were fastening
down whatever might be swept away in a wind and preparing
to leave the ship. All around small boats were pulling to
shore with other seamen. They nearly always camped on shore
when they were in a port.

Some sailors cupped their hands and shouted to him through
the whipping wind, "Go back. Windstorm coming."

Nick would not turn back until he had delivered the papers.
He rowed on, keeping the papers safe and dry. Then, finally

he saw that two seamen were putting out from the silk ship in a rowboat to meet him. With relief he rowed on until the two small boats met, and then he turned over the papers. "A good voyage," he called as they parted.

On his way back, Nicholas battled a gale that blew wilder every moment. Water sloshed on his feet as he steered past an Egyptian ship. Wind screamed from the sea, and his boat scudded toward dangerous rocks. He pulled as hard as he could, and even then barely missed them.

Not another small boat was in sight now. Nick felt small and alone, pulling for shore in his lone little boat among the big, silent ships. He was drenched and very tired when at last he managed to reach the wharf. Stiff with cold and weariness, he climbed the short slippery ladder.

"OOO—ee!" shrieked the wind, as he tied his boat. His cold, wet clothing clung to him, and his teeth chattered.

"Help! Help!"

Nick stiffened. He had heard a cry, but where did it come from? He looked over the bay. There was nothing but churning water and big ships! He decided that he was imagining things. It must be the wind. He started along the wharf.

Above the wind the cry came again. Nick whirled around and examined the bay. This time he saw something by the hidden rocks! A rowboat was foundering! The men in it were fighting the waves and shrieking for help.

Nicholas dashed along the wharf toward town shouting, "Help! Boat on the rocks! Help!" But nobody heard him.

"Help!" he yelled. "Somebody help!" But nobody came. He stared at the small boat battering on the rocks. It pitched

madly and then flung two men into the foaming water.

Shouting "Help!" again, Nicholas ran to his boat and jumped in. Untying it with trembling hands, he made sure the coil of rope was in the boat. Uncle John had used that rope in many a rescue.

Nick shoved off and pulled on the oars. While he rowed, he planned what to do when he reached the struggling men. Whenever he had strength enough, he yelled "Help!" But he had little hope that anyone would hear and come to the rescue.

Then all at once he saw a rowboat leaving a Greek ship! Not every one had gone to shore. Someone else was coming.

Nick was the first to reach the wreck. Wind and waves pounded his boat, almost dashing it on the rocks. An old man struggled in the water, and a young man swam near by. Nick braced himself and threw the rope. The old man missed it, clutching the air desperately; but the young man caught it.

Clinging to the rope, the young man was able to reach the older man and keep him afloat. As they held the rope, Nicholas managed, bit by bit, to row his boat so that they were drawn away from the dangerous whirlpools near the rocks.

Battered by wind, waves, and blinding spray, Nicholas never knew just how the men were saved. Somehow, a big Greek sailor got into Nicholas' boat and together they pulled the old seaman from the water. The other seaman was dragged into another boat before Nick and the big Greek started to row back to shore with the exhausted old man.

"You are brave," said the Greek sailor to Nick. "You keep calm in danger. Some day you will make a good seaman."

Nick smiled, but made no answer. He was too tired to talk.

15

2

The Kings Who Gave
Without Telling

A CROWD GREETED THEM at the wharf. As Nicholas led
the dripping sailors to his home, people clapped him on
the shoulder and chattered all around him.

The sun disappeared behind the mountains. The rough road
was growing dark and hard to follow when a torch shone down
the path. Uncle John had come to look for his boy. He put
his arm around Nicholas and helped him home.

Light streamed from the open doorway as they came to the
house. Anya ran down the path calling, "Nicky! Nicky! Are
you safe?" Brushing people aside, she hugged him. Her tears
splashed on his cheeks. "Oh, Nicky!" she cried, hurrying him
along. "I went to see my cousin, and I stayed too long. When
you did not come home, I was afraid you were drowned."

Once more the people told the tale of the rescue and of
how brave Nicholas was. When she had heard most of it, she

clapped her hands to silence them and snapped, "Nonsense! You will make Nicholas think he is a hero. He is just a boy who acts brave sometimes and makes mistakes often. Come, Nicky, eat your meal."

She led him and the shivering seamen into the warm room. Uncle John bade goodnight to the crowd and closed the door. Then he moved about quietly to find dry clothing for the drenched men. Meanwhile, Anya bustled around setting out food. When Nick, dressed in dry clothes, came down the ladder from his loft under the roof, she was ladling up huge bowls of savory stew.

It tasted good. Pedro, the younger sailor, ate without speaking. Uncle John fed the older man a bit at a time until he could reach for some food himself. No one spoke; everyone ate and rested and got warm inside and out.

Finally, when Pedro was breaking his last piece of crusty bread, he said, "Nicholas, I cannot tell you how thankful I am that you saved our lives."

Nick rumpled his hair, as he often did when he felt self-conscious and did not know what to say. As they talked on about his bravery, he felt more and more uncomfortable. Searching for something to change the conversation, he spied his uncle's writings and a picture on the chest.

"Uncle John, may I show the men the picture you painted?"

The two men crowded close while Nicholas explained that his uncle made copies of stories from the Gospels and illustrated them. The older man nodded, understanding. He had seen writing like this once or twice before, with stories about Jesus. The younger man had never seen such a thing.

The older one explained, "That picture tells the story of the three wise kings who rode from the east to find the Christ Child. See the bright star they are following. How real their camels look, moving through the night toward Bethlehem! This is a beautiful picture."

Nicholas was proud to have his uncle's work praised. He wanted the men to hear the story. "Uncle John, please read to us about the wise men."

Nicholas rested his chin on his hands as his uncle read. The house smelled of ginger and honey-cakes, and was heavy with the smoke of pine wood. He was comfortable and sleepy, but he would not fall asleep during this story. He liked it too much.

While Uncle John read, the lamplight shone on his gray hair and beard and on his thin face scarred by a pirate's sword. The weariness that Nick had seen earlier was gone; the man's eyes shone, and his voice rang clear and glad. He was always this way when people gathered in the room, as they did now, to hear about Jesus.

"Now when Jesus was born in Bethlehem of Judea in the days of Herod the king, behold, wise men from the East came to Jerusalem, saying, 'Where is he who has been born king of the Jews? For we have seen his star in the East and have come to worship him.'"

Nicholas could almost hear the pad-pad of camel's hooves as the kings rode by starlight. Jewels sparkled on their robes. He was worried when they went to see cruel Herod; and he was glad when at last they turned toward Bethlehem.

He smiled happily as Uncle John read, "and, lo, the star which they had seen in the East, went before them til it came to rest over the place where the child was. When they saw the star, they rejoiced exceedingly with great joy; and going into the house, they saw the child with Mary his mother, and they fell down and worshipped him. Then opening their treasures, they offered him gifts, gold and frankincense and myrrh."

For a moment, no one spoke. Then Pedro exclaimed, "What a wonderful story!" He gazed at the picture and then asked, "What were the Kings' names?"

"Their names are not told," Uncle John replied. "They gave their gifts and went away quietly to their homes."

The old sailor nodded. "A good way to give presents." Then he added very softly, "Jesus usually helped people quietly, too."

"He did," Anya agreed.

Later, when the sailors were warmly wrapped in blankets by the fire, and all the house was still, Nicholas climbed the ladder to the loft and opened the small, shuttered window by his bed.

How comfortable it was to lie down! As he lay there, he could see one bright star through the window. That made him think of the wise men who gave presents to Jesus. Frankincense smelled fragrant, especially on festival days; myrrh, with its rich perfume, often was used to ease pain.

And gold! What would it be like to be able to give golden gifts? If he had any gold or silver now, he would give some to the Spanish sailors.

From far away came the sound of camel bells. Perhaps they were part of a caravan carrying gold. He tried to picture it. Before long he did not hear the bells or see the star. He was asleep, dreaming that he traveled toward Bethlehem with the wise kings.

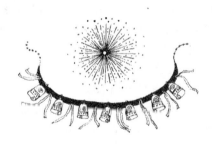

3

Surprise for Nicholas

Next morning Nicholas awoke slowly. From downstairs came the voices of the Spanish sailors thanking Anya once again for the good food she had given them.

"You are welcome," Nick heard her reply. "And may you have a safe journey home."

"I will go to the wharf with you," Uncle John said, as Nicholas listened sleepily. Then as they went out, Nick heard him add, "Let Nicky sleep late this morning. But when he gets up don't forget to tell him that I have a surprise for him."

Anya's voice sounded excited as she replied, "I surely will tell him."

Nicholas yawned and stretched in bed, wondering what surprising thing Uncle John had to show him. Ouch! His back was sore. He had done no rowing during the past winter at school. His school was near the seaport of Myra, but he had very little time to go out on the water of Myra Harbor. He dozed off, wondering what the surprise might be.

When he awoke again, it was to the good smell of baking bread. He turned over to go back to sleep, and then decided to get up and eat some bread while it was warm. He sat up in bed with his blankets around him and yawned.

Anya heard him and called from the foot of the ladder, "Your uncle has a surprise for you when he returns!"

"What kind of surprise?" asked Nick, pulling his clothing on. "It wouldn't be a horse for me to ride, would it, Anya?"

"Nonsense!" she answered. "It certainly would not! Where would your uncle get gold enough to buy you a horse?"

Nicholas jumped down the ladder. What could it be? Maybe it was hidden in the house somewhere. He looked around quickly. Morning sunlight poured through the eastern window, glinting on a small table, on the blanket chest with the copper bowl on it, and on the brick walls of the house. No sign of anything new or different. Where was the surprise?

Anya's black eyes were dancing, but she asked severely, "Nick, did birds nest in your hair this morning? And did you wash your face with soot and ashes?" She pointed sharply toward the well outside.

Anya was not to be argued with, so Nicholas went out and dashed water on his hair and face and into his eyes. It made them tingle. Anya always wanted everything clean.

Three boys from town ran up the road calling, "Nick, they're unloading the spice warehouse."

"I will come after my uncle returns," Nick called back.

The boys waved and ran off. Nicholas looked after them as

he smoothed his wet hair. It was good to have friends. He was glad this was his home. He remembered when he had first come. He had been a lonely little orphan then. He could not remember his parents, and even now was not sure where he had been born. Last year Anya told him that his mother had died during a plague when he was a baby and his father had died shortly after.

The first thing Nicholas could remember was living in a dark, ugly stone house at the edge of a village, with a noisy family who seldom bothered to speak to him. The woman, whose name he now forgot, had fed him and dressed him but never had time to talk kindly with him or play with him. Her children, who were somewhat older than he, had played together and always left him out.

He walked toward his uncle's doorway, recalling how, in the other house, he had felt all alone. The older people sometimes gave surprises and toys to the other children, but he was the child no one remembered——the child who never had a present.

"Your breakfast is ready, Nicky," said Anya. She set a bowl of figs and dates on the table and turned to get bread and goat's milk for him.

"How long must I wait for the surprise?" he asked, munching dates.

"Until you see it." She went out to the well to wash a bowl. Nick suspected she was watching the road from town, to see when Uncle John was coming.

This new surprise couldn't be any greater, he reflected, than his surprise on the day when his uncle came for him at the other house. The woman had shaken his shoulder when he

23

was asleep, crying, "Wake up, Nicholas. We have just heard that your uncle is coming. Get ready quickly. He is going to take you away on a donkey train to live at his house."

Nicholas had loved Uncle John the minute he saw him.

Anya bustled indoors as Nicholas sat dreaming of the past. "I want to get things cleared up before your uncle returns," she said.

"Please tell me about the surprise," he begged. "I can hardly wait."

"Nonsense!" she snapped. "Anyone can wait for a surprise if he has to."

Just then Uncle John strode in smiling, tossed his cloak on a bench, and went straight to a corner of the wall. "Now for the surprise, Nicky!"

Without a word, Anya began to help Uncle John remove some bricks from the wall. Why were they doing that? Nick wondered. What was in there? He could hardly wait to see and started to pull some bricks out himself; but Anya stopped him with a glance.

Nick backed up and stood waiting, breathless, while Uncle John reached way into the wall. Slowly he pulled out a leather bag. Something in it clinked. "What's in that bag?" Nick cried. No one answered. Instead his Uncle John moved toward the table.

Almost overcome with curiosity, Nicholas followed close on his uncle's heels. He wanted to help untie the leather thong, but Anya pushed his hands aside. At last Uncle John tipped the bag, and a stream of gold and silver coins poured onto the table!

Nicholas gasped, speechless. Never had he seen so much money. It tumbled into a shining heap before his astonished eyes.

Uncle John said, "This is all yours, Nicky."

"Mine!" Nick's voice was a high squeak of surprise.

Anya spoke up briskly, "All yours. Your uncle has been guarding it for you. This bagful will pay for your education." She paused, smiling broadly. Then she added in a loud whisper, "When you are grown you will receive more bags of gold and silver. You will be a very rich man some day."

"Me! A rich man?"

"Very rich; but do not get big ideas because you have money." Then, in spite of her gruff words, Anya gently pushed him toward the table. "Touch your money. It won't bite you." She filled his hands with gold and silver pieces that sparkled in the sunlight. He ran them through his fingers—clink, clink. His eyes were dazzled by the glint and glitter of the coins.

"Where did it come from?" he asked wonderingly.

Uncle John put his hand on Nicholas' shoulder. "Your father left this gold and silver for you before he died. He was a fine man—rich and generous. Your mother, who was my little sister, was lovely. It is sad that you were left an orphan so young!"

Nicholas slowly picked up two handfuls of silver and gold pieces. So these were presents from his mother and father, who had not lived long enough to give him presents such as other children had. He blinked back salty tears. He must not make Uncle John and Anya sad now. Besides, this was surely a surprise, the like of which he had never dreamed. And more to come when he was older! Maybe some day he could buy a swift horse.

"What shall I do with all my money?" he asked, slowly dropping some back into the bag, piece by piece.

Uncle John answered, "The fortune you receive after you are grown will be yours to use in any way you think best. As Anya said, the gold and silver in this bag will pay your school expenses for years to come. It should be handed to Brother Simeon of your school as soon as possible, so that he can take care of it for you. I had planned to ride back to school with you tomorrow and take it to him; but several people need my help, and I cannot go."

"I will take the money," Nicholas offered, holding a coin to the light and flashing its reflection on the opposite wall. "We could put this leather bag in the big sack of other things I'm taking back with me."

"You!" Anya exclaimed. "Take that money alone on the donkey train?" She looked down at him as if he were a foolish puppy. "Wouldn't you be afraid?"

"Me? Afraid!" Nicholas spoke with his most booming voice and stood as tall as he could—which wasn't very tall because he was short for his age. "I would not be afraid to take ten times this much gold and silver all the way to Egypt!"

Anya snorted, and Nicholas lost his great, big voice. He tried to explain naturally. "It's not as if Myra were far away, Anya. Besides, I know Marcus and his father who drive the donkey train. I'll ask them to let me off at the top of the hill by the little footpath that leads down through the ravine and up to the school."

Anya still was not convinced. But all she said was, "My brave young traveler, do not tell everyone on the donkey train that you are carrying a small fortune."

"I won't tell anyone," Nicholas answered meekly, and then grinned as she stopped his talk by popping a honey-ginger cake into his mouth.

As he chewed, he dropped the coins one by one into the bag. They clinked merrily in, all but the last one. It rolled under a bench. Scrambling for it, Nick knocked his uncle's cloak to the floor. For the first time he noticed how old and shabby it was!

Nicholas held it to the light and cried, "Uncle John, I want to buy you a new cloak. This is worn thin. You never buy anything for yourself."

A smile lighted Uncle John's face. He was pleased. "You are very kind, Nicky," he said. "I thank you. However, this cloak is good enough for me."

"Please, Uncle John I never had money to buy a present for you before."

"My boy, it is enough that you really want to buy it."

"Nicho-laus!" Anya called from the shed, where she had gone on an errand. "Come sweep up these walnuts."

He ran to the shed, flinging his uncle's cloak on a woodpile back of the door. "Anya, I'm sorry!" he said, scooping together some of the walnuts he had spilled and broken the day before. "I meant to do this yesterday. I forgot."

"Always forgetting!" she grumbled as she went back indoors.

Later, Uncle John and Nick agreed that he would take a small part of the gold and silver with him when he returned to school.

The rest would be sent with a gold caravan. The school Nick went to was small. It was taught by a good Christian man. There were few such schools and most of them were poor. Good Brother Simeon could use Nicholas' money well.

Together Nick and his uncle counted out twenty-five pieces of silver and ten pieces of gold, and put them in a small leather bag. "There," said Uncle John, "that will be enough to take with you now." Then he told Nicholas to go down to Patara and ask the agent of the gold caravan to have the caravan take the rest of the gold and silver to Brother Simeon next time it went to Myra.

Uncle John put his arm around Nicholas' shoulders and looked down at his nephew kindly. "You know, Nick, I am getting old. Within a few years I may give up the Patara church to a younger man. I want to leave all your affairs in good order, and I know they will be taken care of well by Brother Simeon until you are old enough to manage for yourself."

Nicholas did not hear everything his uncle said. All he heard was that Uncle John might leave Patara some day. "What will you do if you are not pastor here?" he cried.

Uncle John looked happy. "For almost two hundred years learned men have been studying the Gospel stories and the other writings about Jesus; and they are coming to agree that many of these should be gathered together. I may be able to help."

"Oh!" Nicholas exclaimed, glad for Uncle John. "Will you teach young men how to copy the stories about Jesus and how to illustrate them?"

"That is what I would like to do," Uncle John agreed. "Although scribes have been making copies of books for centuries, only lately have the stories of Jesus been copied in any number."

They talked together for some time about this great plan. "It is wonderful," said Nicky, imagining people listening to the Gospel in churches and schools in Asia and Africa and as far away as Spain.

Before starting for town Nicholas took the bag of coins back to the hiding place in the wall. Just as he was sliding it in, he had an idea. When he was in the market place, he would buy a sack of walnuts to replace those he had spilled and a jar of honey because he had broken one. And he would pay for them with his own money!

He took a silver coin from the bag, trying to act as if he did that sort of thing every day. As he slid the leather bag back into its niche, he began to whistle softly. It was a comfortable thing to have money of one's own.

4

Thaddeus' Misfortune

NICHOLAS stepped out into the sunny morning and glanced down at the bay. A gentle breeze puffed the sails as sailors hoisted them for the springtime sailings. He hoped Thaddeus' ship was making good headway at sea. Thinking of the ship and tossing and catching his coin in the air, he swung along downhill toward the market place.

First he stopped at the busy inn. He went to the room where the agent for the caravan was and explained about the money.

The agent, an Arabian, was making a note of it when a terrible noise shattered the air. Nicholas and the agent ran outside to look. In a cloud of dust a caravan raced to the inn, drivers yelling, camels snorting, bells jangling wildly, and people running from everywhere shouting, "What has happened?"

Somehow the caravan stopped without trampling anyone. And above the hubbub of jostling people Nick heard a camel-driver cry, "Pirates! Thaddeus' ship! They've captured it!"

There was silence as the chief driver told the tale. Nicholas' arms prickled with horror.

At dawn the caravan had been traveling through a fishing village to the west and a fisherman had come, shouting the news that Thaddeus' ship had been captured by pirates during the night. The caravan had traveled on another mile until the men spied two pirate ships in a nearby cove. Then the drivers had turned their camels around and fled back to Patara to get more guards.

Nobody paid much attention to the end of the tale. As soon as people heard about Thaddeus' ship, they felt that they had heard the worst. "He is ruined!" women wailed. Our good nobleman and his wife! What will become of their poor little daughters?"

Nicholas stood still. This was a terrible misfortune for Thaddeus! Then Nick remembered the seamen and the ship's captain. Were they prisoners of the pirates, as Uncle John had been? Nick worked his way through the crowd and asked one of the drivers about the silk ship's crew.

"They escaped in small boats while the pirates plundered the ship. They put up a brave fight to drive the pirates off, but it was useless," the driver answered. "All of them landed safely in the fishing village just before we reached it."

Nicholas went home very low spirited. At the door he saw that Anya was weeping. She had heard the news when one of the caravan drivers came to tell Uncle John. "Our nobleman is penniless," she kept repeating. "His little girls will starve. They will have no dowries." She wiped her tears with the back of her hand and tried to stop crying. "Your uncle has gone to break the bad news to Thaddeus. Everything has gone wrong. I could not even find your uncle's cloak, although I looked everywhere."

"Don't cry, Anya. I'll find the cloak and take it up to him so he can wear it home." He patted her shoulder. Then he looked under the table and in the blanket chest and on the pegs on the wall. Next he stepped to the shed, although Anya muttered, "Your uncle never leaves his clothes there." But there was the cloak, back of the door where Nick had tossed it.

As Nicholas started with the cloak uphill to Thaddeus' house he wondered why Anya was worrying about the dowries. He knew it was the custom, especially in wealthy and noble families, for parents to begin when each daughter was young to gather a sum of money, fine clothing, linen, silver and such things. When the girl married, she took this dowry with her to her husband's home. But Thaddeus' daughters were too young to marry.

"Poof!" said Nicholas to himself. "It is much too soon for Anya to worry about dowries for Thaddeus' daughters. They're hardly more than babies!"

Nick had not been up to the house of Thaddeus for a whole year, not since just before he went away to school in Myra. Now he saw that the fences about the land were broken. Evidently Thaddeus did not have much of a flock or many servants to keep his land in order.

Nick went on through a pine wood; and then through a clearing he saw a handsome marble archway with wrought-iron gates, and beyond it the big house. It needed repair. Tiles were

33

missing from the roof, and one end of the house had no roof at all. It had been destroyed by a fire that raged through the forest and down the mountainside twenty years before.

Nicholas walked through the gateway and up to the door. He had never been inside the house before.

Uncle John came to let him in. "It is good you came, Nicky. Thaddeus and I want to go together to talk with his wife about what has happened. She is not well and is resting in her room. The servant is not here right now. Will you stay in the court and take care of the little girls?"

Nicholas was startled. He did not know how to take care of little children. Before he could answer, Thaddeus greeted him. The man's face was haggard, but he held himself tall and straight as always and smiled a real welcome. "I have not seen you in more than a year, Nicholas. Thank you for taking those papers to the ship. It was kind of you to do it for me."

Two little girls were clinging to their father. He perched one on each shoulder, saying of the older, "This is Thekla. She is four." Thekla brushed back her golden curls and looked at Nicholas with big, serious blue eyes.

From the other shoulder, a round-cheeked little one swooped forward laughing and pulled Nick's hair. He caught her chubby hand and loosened it from his hair while her brown eyes bubbled with mischief as she tried to pull away. Her father could not help smiling. "This is Elena. She is nearly two." She pulled her own brown hair in all directions, chirruping like a plump, saucy bird planning new mischief. Her face was smudged and her tunic muddy, but she did not care.

On a couch in the corner, the little baby, Carita, slept soundly.

"Nicholas," his uncle asked again, "you will take care of the children so we may talk quietly?"

Nick murmured, "Yes, Uncle John," and hoped the men would not be gone long. As soon as they left, Elena cried, and Thekla stood sadly by the baby's bed. Nicholas realized that if the two older girls awakened the baby, he'd have three children on his hands. What could he do to make them happy? He tried making faces. Elena howled. He stood on his head. That made things worse.

Then he remembered how Uncle John had played horse with him when he was small. So he crawled on the floor, saying, "I'm a horse. Do you want a ride?"

The little girls came at once. Thekla helped Elena on and held her while Nick crawled up and down the court. He could

see that originally the mosaics on this floor had been beautiful, but now they were broken and in several places tiles were lost. The floor was bare, except for one large and very handsome rug. Anya had told Nicholas about this rug. It was one of the finest in the region. All of the others in the house had been sold.

"Please, may I ride now?" Thekla spoke gently to her little sister. Soon Thekla was riding while Elena trotted along, swatting Nicholas to make him go faster. They rode and rode, taking turns, until Elena grew weary and whimpered. Nicholas looked for their toys, but found none. Elena whimpered louder. What should he do? He saw a chunk of pine wood by the hearth, and that gave him an idea.

"Thekla," he said, "if you will sit here, I will make you each a toy horse."

The children crowded together into their father's carved chair while Nicholas sat on the floor. As he whittled, he made up a story about a toy pony. The girls were quiet and interested. Soon Elena got her horse. She hugged it to her and patted its back.

Nick was just finishing the second horse when the men returned. The little girls scrambled from the chair to show the toys to their father. Thaddeus was pleased and thanked Nicholas. Being thanked for something he had done always made Nicholas uncomfortable. Rumpling his hair, he said politely, "You are very welcome," and hurried to follow his uncle home.

As they went out through the gateway, he exclaimed to Uncle John, "What a fine-looking man Thaddeus is! Friendly and pleasant, too! But he is tired and worried."

Uncle John agreed. "He has much to worry about. He is deeply in debt because of his silk ship; and he is so proud and honest he vows he will pay every bit he owes and nobody will suffer because of his losses."

"Could I give him some of my gold? I'd be glad to." Nicholas was excited about the idea.

"No!" Uncle John spoke positively. "Today I offered him what I have and whatever I could raise to help him take care of his family. But he is very independent. He was grateful but would not accept such help. He declares he will find some way to earn money to repay every debt and provide for his family as well."

Nicholas stopped short in the road. He insisted that he had more money than he needed. "We must persuade him to take some."

Uncle John shook his head. "I am glad you want to share

37

your good fortune, Nicky; but do not even try to give any of your gold to Thaddeus. He would refuse."

They walked the rough downhill road in silence. Nicky kicked a pebble. If only he could think of some way to help Thaddeus.

"There goes the Spanish ship toward the harbor mouth," Uncle John exclaimed. "The weather has settled, and this breeze is right for a good start."

Lifting aside a pine branch that brushed his face, Nicholas asked, "Uncle John, do you think Pedro will tell others the story of the three kings?"

"He will, Nick." As they drew nearer home, Uncle John added, "And those he tells will tell others. That is the way the word spreads."

5

Nicholas
and the Robbers

NEXT MORNING Nicholas' uncle awakened him as dawn touched the bay with soft, rosy light. It was the day to start back to school. Nick groaned. It was not that he disliked school, but it made him sad to leave home.

As usual, Anya covered her feelings with extra scoldings. When Nick went downstairs, she was putting a new tunic she had woven for him into the big sack he would take back to school and muttering that she knew it would be in rags soon because he was so careless with his clothes. He saw, however, that she was dropping in oranges, too, and nuts. There was a mound of spicy cakes wrapped in a clean cloth for him to take, besides the lunch he would eat on the way.

He got the bag of coins and, with Uncle John's help, settled it in the big sack. Anya kept warning him not to let anyone know he had it, and he merely answered, "Yes, Anya."

39

"Here comes the donkey train: Hurry!" Anya cried at last. She scurried out to tell the driver that Nicholas was riding to Myra. Nick and his uncle tossed the rest of his things into the sack—a ball, his flute, and the lunch—and hurried out to greet Marcus and his father.

While Nick and his uncle stowed the sack in the saddlebag on the little brown donkey Nick would ride, Anya came over to retell the bad news she had just heard. She got all the news from every donkey train that passed. "Thaddeus sold his last rug this morning. It is on this train with other rugs to be shipped from Myra by a Spanish rug-merchant."

"His last rug sold!" Nick exclaimed. He mounted his donkey sadly.

Soon the train jingled and jogged through the misty early morning down a bypath that led back of Patara's market place. "No use stopping there today," Marcus explained, riding close to Nick. "We have no more room." He lowered his voice. "I hope robbers or pirates do not find out that we are carrying a fortune in rugs."

Nick kept still, but he remembered the gold and silver he carried. They will not take my fortune away from me, he thought.

He gave Patara one last look. There would be few school holidays from now on. He could see his uncle's house on the hill and beyond it, farther up, the house of Thaddeus. It made him feel sad to see the nobleman's old house. He wished he could help. He wondered for a moment how he might do it, then he turned his attention to the way ahead.

The road led close to the sea. Nicholas felt the sack in his

saddlebag quietly and thought of·the pirates and the silk ship. Marcus, who was glancing beyond hastily in all directions, remarked, "I guess there are no pirates along this shore. Those fishermen would not be mending their nets so peacefully if there were."

As the train traveled on, pine-covered mountains rose from near the water's edge. The sea lapped close to the donkey's feet. Nick and Marcus waved to people walking the dusty road from village to village. Morning passed into noon. The donkeys trotted down a lane to a short wharf near a small village. There lay the boat that carried things from one coastal village to another and to big ships in the seaports.

Marcus leaped from his donkey and ran ahead to tell about the pirates and Thaddeus' misfortune. Everyone flocked around, chattering in sympathy and shouting against the pirates. "Back to work," the owner of the boat finally ordered, and the loading continued.

While the donkeys rested and ate, Nicholas and Marcus shared their bread and cheese and oranges and some cakes, and watched the boat.

On the road again, the donkeys trotted mile after mile, their jingling bells ringing through sunny hillsides and groves of gnarled olive trees. In some fields farmers were plowing the earth, still damp with recent rains. On and on the train moved, past miles of white sandy beaches and sheltered coves. Every turn in the road brought delightful sights—orange groves, terraced vineyards, and fig trees and olive trees. Nicholas enjoyed it all.

However, as the afternoon sped, he wished he was at school

with his money. He and Marcus shared more bread and cheese, for he would be too late for supper. Too late, also, to hear Brother Simeon's story at vesper time. Brother Simeon was easygoing, and though a great scholar, he always talked in a way the boys could understand. And he enjoyed everyday things, like walking in the woods and watching birds.

Nicholas liked the stories Brother Simeon read. When he told about the time Jesus' friends were frightened during a storm at sea, his plain face beamed and his voice boomed as he asked the questions Jesus had asked the terrified men. "Why are you frightened? Where is your faith?" That was a good story, Nick thought, as they jogged on.

Already the donkeys threw long shadows on the road. The afternoon grew dim as they reached a hilltop from which Nick could look down on Myra Harbor. Ships were misty with coming nightfall. It would be hard to see a pirate ship hiding in a cove, and the pirates could swarm up quickly from the shore to overtake travelers.

He looked down at Myra, with its many buildings and large amphitheater. Now that night was coming he wished he could ride to the city and wait in the busy market place for someone from school to meet him. Suddenly the mountains hid the sun, and darkness fell.

The donkeys stopped by a dark grove of trees. Nicholas got off slowly and called good-by in a big, brave voice to Marcus and his father. Before long the donkey train was a far-off jingle. Slinging his sack over his shoulder, Nick slipped and slid down a path that led through a gloomy ravine, thick with cypress trees. His school was in a house on the other side of the ravine and

43

beyond a meadow. He kept looking around. Robbers might be following. He heard twigs snapping and hid behind a tree. It might be pirates.

When all was still again, he ran down the path toward a brook. He would cross quickly on the log and run uphill among the trees, then over the meadow to school. Something moved again. Maybe there were robbers with a hide-out in this ravine. They moved again! Twigs snapped. Nick fled back up the path down which he had just come, stumbling over rolling stones. His heart pounded too hard to hear if the robbers were chasing him. But he had to rest a minute! He was panting hard. His sack was heavy. He crawled into a thicket and lay gasping for breath, scared and alone.

Across the ravine, dark figures still moved mysteriously under the trees. Nick didn't dare leave the thicket. The night was cold. What would Brother Simeon think if he did not return tonight?

Nicholas sat up. "Why are you afraid? Where is your faith?" He could not expect God to help him if he hid here, cowering under a bush.

He got up, shouldered his sack, and grabbed a stick. He was determined to make so much noise that the robbers, or pirates, or whatever they were, would think he was a crowd of people. Flailing the stick, he ran downhill shouting, "Come on, everybody. Catch these robbers and pirates."

Zigzagging back and forth, he kept yelling in all sorts of voices so as to sound like a dozen people. He crossed the brook and charged wildly up the hill, shouting at the mysterious figures.

44

"Maaa-aa!" they bleated, angry and surprised, and galloped
into the clearing and across the
meadow toward school. Nicholas stood still, staring open-
mouthed. Three goats! And he
had accused them of being robbers or pirates.

He laughed at himself all the
way across the meadow and up
to the door of the big gray stone
house. He flung open the door
with a bang. Trying to catch
the door, he tipped his heavy
sack. Oranges, nuts, cakes, and
clothes rolled over the floor.
Boys scrambled for the food,
crying, "Nicholas is here, strew-
ing things around as usual."

Waving to them, he hurried
toward Brother Simeon's small
room at the back of the school,
thankful he hadn't spilled his
silver and gold. "I must give
Brother Simeon a message from
my uncle," Nick called to the
boys.

In a few minutes the money
was safe with the good teacher.

"I will take good care of your money and pay your expenses with it," the Brother said. "If you need some at any time, tell me."

"I don't know what I would need it for," Nicholas said. Then he remembered to thank his teacher for taking care of the money.

As he was saying goodnight, Brother Simeon said, "A new boy came two days ago. He's only five years old, and he's lonely. He is asleep now. We put him in the bed near the door so he can see the light in the hall at night. He's an orphan. Maybe you can cheer him up because you remember how it feels to be a lonely orphan."

"I certainly do, sir," Nicholas answered.

By the time he reached the big room where all the boys' beds were, most of the boys were asleep. Nicholas tiptoed into the dim room, past Galfu's bed. Galfu was a big boy. If anyone bothered him, he got angry and shouted. He was always complaining or carrying tales, or taking things away from the smaller boys.

Not far from Galfu, the new little boy huddled in bed. His covers were pulled around his ears. What a small one he was!

Nicholas was almost asleep when he heard muffled sobbing. He sat up and listened. It was the little orphan. Galfu stirred and snarled, "Keep still!" The crying stopped. Nicholas lay awake a long time. It was hard to be a lonely little orphan. But there ought to be some way to make the child happy. Maybe a surprise toy! But where would Nick get one? He thought for a while, but he couldn't think of anything; he was too sleepy.

Then he remembered the toys he had made for Elena and

Thekla. Soon he was tiptoing among the silent sleepers. In the wood basket he found a piece of wood from which he could make a toy goat as soon as dawn came.

When the first sunbeams blinked through the open windows, Nicholas was awake. Deftly he whittled the toy. Before long, it really began to look like a goat. He worked fast to get it done before the others awoke. No one must know who gave the gift.

As soon as the little beast was finished, Nicholas crept toward the small boy's bed and hid it in his sandal. Then Nick sped back and sprang into his own bed. He sprang so hard that he crashed to the floor on the other side.

Boys woke suddenly, crying, "What's that noise?"

In the hubbub nobody noticed Nick crawling sheepishly back into his bed, for he was shouting with the rest, "What's that noise?"

Brother Simeon came in to quiet them down. Since they were all wide awake, he suggested that they get dressed.

Nicholas watched as the little lad reached down for his shoes. He put his foot into one and fastened it wearily. Then he belted his tunic and almost did not bother about his other shoe.

Galfu tripped over it and growled, "Get that thing out of here!" He kicked the shoe across the room, and the frightened child scurried after it. A boy close by picked it up and went to help the little one put it on. Then they both called out in surprise, "A toy goat! In the sandal!"

The boys came crowding around, "How did it get there? Who gave it to you?"

Nobody seemed to know. "Maybe it was Brother Simeon," someone whispered.

"It's a friendly goat," the little boy declared proudly. "I'll let you play with it," he said to another small child who stood watching.

Then the big boy who had found the sandal had an idea. "Let us big ones make toy animals for the younger ones. We could make them each a different kind of animal, and they could play Noah's ark."

"I'm hungry," Galfu complained. "Let's go to breakfast."

"Nicky," one of his friends said, teasing, "your fingers fumble, but you can make something very simple. Maybe the roof of the ark."

Nicholas grinned and agreed. "Someone will have to show me how."

A crash in the front hall sent everyone running to see what was happening. "Goats!" someone yelled. Three goats frisked through the hall, butting over benches and small tables. Nicholas was one of the boys who herded the goats outside, while other boys picked up furniture.

There was so much confusion that nobody heard Nick calling to the goats as, laughing, he chased them downhill. "Run to your hide-out in the ravine! You pirates! You robbers!"

6

Nicholas Chooses Well

T HE YEARS PASSED quickly. Although Nicholas was unable to go home, he and his uncle wrote long letters to each other. Uncle John wrote that the lovely wife of Thaddeus had died. Anya now went there frequently to help, because all of the servants were gone. Nick was sorry that the little girls were without a mother, but he knew Anya would be good to them.

Another letter brought more bad news. Carita's left foot was injured. She had to walk with a crutch. Thaddeus was poorer than ever, and spent whatever he could for doctors, to try to cure Carita.

On reading this, Nicholas wrote at once to his uncle that he wanted to give Thaddeus some gold.

"Nicholas, it is useless to offer Thaddeus part of your fortune," Uncle John replied, "much as you want to help him. He will accept nothing." Nick was disappointed.

There was a short note from Anya, too. As he unrolled it, Nick marveled at the way his uncle had been able to teach her to read and write. Few people could read and write. And certainly very few women!

Her letter started Nick thinking. She said, just as Uncle John had, that there was no use in trying to give a present to Thaddeus. "But," she added, "someday you may find a way to help him without his knowing who gives the gift. Or, at the right time, you may make a secret gift to his daughters. If you do, tell no one—not even me."

Nick had little time, however, to ponder this problem; for every month there seemed to be more work at school. Nicholas enjoyed games and good times with his friends, and there were times when he played more than he should. But on the whole, he worked hard.

So it was that one day Brother Simeon selected Nicholas and two other boys to go to Myra two days a week to help the Bishop. The Bishop of Myra was in charge of the Myra Cathedral and of all nearby Christian churches. He did a great deal of good among the poor; and since he was old, he needed young helpers to visit poor families in the area and take them food and clothing.

The work was hard. Never before had Nicholas realized how many poor and lonely people there were. Whatever he did seemed so very little when there was so much need in the world. But when he spoke of this to the Bishop, the old man answered, "Each one of us must do our very best and trust in God as Jesus did. Who knows how many people are happier because of one kindhearted deed? It is like lighting a candle in the dark.

One candle brightens the night for many people. And some light more candles from it, to carry shining to others."

So Nicholas forgot about himself and how little he could do, and did his very best to brighten the lives of those people he could help. Often he wondered what he should do when he became a man—what work to choose. Slowly, he came to realize that it must be something that would help other people.

In time he decided to work for the church, helping God take care of people as his uncle and Brother Simeon and the Bishop did. Both Simeon and the Bishop were happy about Nicholas' decision. They began making plans.

Brother Simeon said, "You will need more time to work at the Cathedral, especially with poor children. Children like you, and they try to do what is right when you show them how."

The Bishop agreed, adding, "The donkey train goes to Patara today. You must visit your uncle and tell him of your plans. He has some plans, too, which I have helped him work out A younger pastor will take the Patara church, and your Uncle John will go to Egypt."

"Egypt?" echoed Nicholas.

"In Egypt scholars are studying early Christian writings and helping collect them so that people hundreds of years from now will be able to read and understand about Jesus' way of life," the Bishop explained.

"Uncle John will be very happy helping to do that," Nicholas replied, pleased and proud of his uncle. And he hurried off to catch the donkey train to Patara.

Marcus, who now drove the train, was just starting the lead donkey when Nicholas dashed up, panting. Nick tripped over a

sleeping dog and plunged into a fruit stall. Oranges, pomegranates, and apricots, flew in all directions. The fruit vendor scolded; dogs yelped; donkeys brayed; children came running and shouting; and everyone scrambled for fruit.

Nicholas begged the vendor to forgive him. "I am such a clumsy one," he admitted. "I always leap before I look. My feet will never learn to move quietly and carefully." He took several silver pieces from the leather purse in his belt and put them in the man's hand. "This will pay for the fruit. Let the children enjoy it. I cannot pay you for the confusion I caused."

In a moment, everyone in the market was laughing goodnaturedly at the awkward young man whose feet would not move quietly and carefully. Smiling and munching fruit, the children waved the donkey train on its way.

Nicholas rode close to Marcus; and the two old friends exchanged news as they jogged along. Marcus said that Anya planned to live at the nobleman's house after Uncle John left Patara. "She never stops worrying about dowries for his daughters when they grow up. What will they do? Such fine young women cannot marry without a dowry."

Nicholas nodded in agreement. As he stroked his little donkey's ears, he remarked, "Six years have passed since I have seen Thaddeus' family. Perhaps I would not recognize them, and surely they have forgotten me."

"It is a fine family," Marcus said. "If only some persons of great wealth could be found to give the daughters dowries when they reach marriageable age! Sometimes that happens. But you and I could never find such a person." He laughed and tapped the lead donkey's sides, and all the beasts trotted briskly.

Nicholas laughed, too. "How could we ever find anyone with a fortune who wanted to give it away? And the day is too fair for us to be gloomy about other people's troubles. Let us sing as we ride."

Through the morning sunlight they jogged, singing lilting songs together. And when they rested at noon, all the travelers shared their food and shared, too, stories and legends from the many lands they had seen.

The tales from far and near continued as they rode on in the afternoon. But even though he listened eagerly, Nicholas kept watching for familiar sights. At last they drew near Patara. From a distance he could see his little home, perched on the hillside beyond the town. There was the fig tree by the door and the olive trees beyond. He was too far away to see the flowers growing down the hillside to the shore, but he knew the grass was sprinkled with pink and purple, blue and yellow.

It seemed like a long time before the donkey train finally reached the center of the busy town. But as soon as it did, Nicholas jumped off his donkey and, calling, "Good-by," ran up the hill.

Anya and Uncle John were surprised and delighted.

Anya looked the same to Nick; but Uncle John seemed much older. After supper they sat outside and talked. When Nicholas told about his plans for his life work, Uncle John was happy.

He said, "Nicky, the world is large. The sun and moon shine down on millions of people, and most of them want to live peacefully. But many need to learn how to get along happily together. Remind everyone you can, 'Blessed are the peacemakers, for they shall be called the children of God.' I am sure that you will spread peace and good will wherever you are."

Uncle John stood up. "Nicky, come inside. I shall give you a lifelong treasure."

Nick kept wondering what it could be, as they walked into the lamplit house. Not gold or silver, surely. But what lifelong treasure?

From a big chest, his uncle began taking rolls of books and handing them to Nick. "Here are some of the Christian scriptures, Nicky, that I have been copying for years, letters from church leaders and stories of Jesus. These are books which our Christian leaders are planning to put together and preserve." He looked directly at his nephew. "Read them often and help others to understand the teachings so they may live good, useful, happy lives."

Nicholas hardly knew what to say, he was so grateful for this gift that represented years of his uncle's life. At last he simply thanked his uncle and promised to use the writings wisely and guard them faithfully.

Uncle John pointed out some of the writing. "There is the story of the Apostle Paul. It tells that as he was making his last voyage to Jerusalem he sailed to Rhodes and then to Patara. Here in our seaport he and his friends found a ship sailing to the coast of Phoenicia, not many miles north of Jerusalem."

Nicholas read the account with interest. Then he said, "Uncle John, I want to go to the Holy Land some day and see the little town of Bethlehem where Jesus was born."

"Nick, I hope you can go. Bethlehem has not changed much since Jesus was born nearly three hundred years ago; but his good news that God loves all people and wants to help them has traveled to many lands and changed many people and places for the better. Christian churches are in countless places."

"But not all Christian churches are safe," Nicholas replied. "Brother Simeon says the emperor has tortured many Christians. We've heard stories about brave Christian martyrs who were persecuted and killed by earlier emperors, and Brother Simeon says that some day we may have to suffer if we are loyal to our faith."

"That is true," Uncle John answered. "If persecution comes, we must be brave for God."

"I will try to be brave and loyal," Nicholas promised.

"Indeed," he went on to say as he carefully gathered the writings together and rolled them in a soft sheepskin, "I hope and pray that in time of danger I shall be brave enough to protect these words that show people the best way to live." He dreaded to think that soon the persecution of Christians might come to their province. But he knew it was possible.

There was little time to talk during the next few days. Time was spent packing Uncle John's things and getting the house ready for the new pastor. Nicholas borrowed a handcart and filled it with the belongings Uncle John was taking to Egypt. He was not taking much—just a few clothes, writing tools, and the chest with the writings he had not given to Nicholas.

Neighbors wanted to help with the work, but Anya would not let them. "You'll only get underfoot," she told them; but they understood that she wanted to be alone with Nicholas and Uncle John as they cleared out their old home.

When the three of them started down to the wharf to see Uncle John off, people came from all sides and walked along silently, trying to let their old pastor know how much they would miss him. Nicholas was sad, for he and his uncle might

56

never see each other again. He tried to smile as he pushed the cart, bumping downhill over the rocky road. He did not want to sadden Uncle John and Anya.

Nick stowed the things in the small boat that would carry Uncle John to the large ship he was to sail away in. Uncle John got in, greeted the seaman who would row him out, and then turned to wave farewell to Nicholas and Anya.

As they stood on the wharf waving farewell, the small boat pulled away. Anya's tears splashed down her cheeks. Nicholas felt a salty taste on his lips, too. They did not talk much as they returned to the empty house.

7

Thaddeus' Family

NICK PICKED UP the sack that held Anya's belongings and slung it over his shoulder. His back bent beneath the heavy load as they started the upward climb to Thaddeus' house where Anya would live now.

She walked beside him, carrying her broom and a basket with odds and ends—some salt, some spices, and other small household treasures. They both tried to think of things that would take their minds off of the parting with Uncle John.

"It's about six years," Nick remarked, "since I have been to Thaddeus' house. Maybe no one will recognize me."

"You were a boy then," Anya answered, "and now you are a man. The girls were little ones then. Now Thekla is ten, and Elena, eight. Carita is six. She cannot walk without a crutch; but she manages well."

As they drew near the house, a big ram burst through the

gateway, with a rosy-cheeked girl chasing after. Spying Anya, she cried, "Catch the ram, please."

"We'll get him, Elena," Anya called. She picked up a broken pine branch and used it to head the ram toward some bushes. "Grab its horns, Nicky," she ordered.

He did. He held tight so as not to get bucked. Quickly Elena knelt in the dust beside the big shaggy animal. She patted its rough back, talking comfortingly and promising to be gentle if he would stand still while she removed a thorn from its hoof. "Good old Giant," she kept saying. The ram seemed to understand and stood quietly.

Swiftly, she pulled out the thorn. Then the ram leaped up, tossed Nick into the bushes, and galloped away leaving Elena sprawling, but unhurt, in the dust. She picked herself up, laughing as she brushed back her glossy brown hair. Her round cheeks were smudged, her skirt torn; but this did not trouble her. The ram was all right.

Seeing her father with Thekla and Carita coming toward the gateway, she called, "Anya has come. The young man who carried her things is very strong. He held Giant by the horns."

The nobleman came forward, recognizing Nicholas at once. Thekla followed with Carita, who limped slowly. Thaddeus welcomed Nicholas, explaining to his daughters, "This is our friend Nicholas, who made the toy horses when you were little."

Thekla greeted Nicholas with a gentle smile. "We still have those horses," she said in a low sweet voice. Nicholas would have known her anywhere because of her golden hair and her eyes as blue as the sky.

At first Carita stood close to her father, looking up at Nicholas with soft brown eyes, and saying not a word. But after a while when they went to see a little bird with a hurt wing, she forgot to be shy. She took Nicholas' hand and said, "Come, see the nest we made in a basket."

While the girls chirped to the bird and fed it crumbs, Nicholas stood with their father watching them. "Three more different sisters never were," Thaddeus said fondly. "Thekla is always polite, even-tempered, quiet, and kind. Elena is noisy, and rough and tumble; but she has a soft heart, especially for anything that has been hurt. Carita is timid and frail; yet she does not complain because she cannot run as the others do. Of course, at times they are all naughty little girls."

However, Nick saw none of the naughtiness that afternoon. They became real friends with him and took him all around. They showed him a waterfall near the house, and a tame deer, and the flock of sheep. Giant, whose horns Nick had held, "baa-aaed" loudly at the sight of them and scrambled away over rocks, with the rest of the flock following. It seemed to Nicholas like a very small flock.

Evening came too soon. Thaddeus and his daughters urged Nicholas to stay overnight at their home, but he had arranged to go to Myra that night by a camel caravan.

"Will you please come to see us soon again, Nicholas?" Carita begged.

Anya spoke quickly. "He will come when he can. Some day you will call him Father Nicholas, for he is planning to become a priest of the church."

Elena exclaimed, "He will be a good Father Nicholas. Everybody will like him."

As they walked a short way down the road with him, Carita said softly, "Do not forget us."

"I will never forget you," he promised. "We will always be friends, even though I will not be able to visit you very often."

That night as he rode a swaying camel along the Myra road, he thought of the family in the shabby old house. He wished he knew of some way to lighten the kind nobleman's burdens. Although Thaddeus smiled often at his little girls, he was very wan and sad-looking when he thought no one was looking.

Great Honors for Nicholas

M UCH WORK awaited Nicholas in Myra. Day after day he
studied hard; and he visited the sick and the poor for
many miles around. He made friends with children who lived
in lonely huts perched on rocky hillsides, or in cottages nestled
along the shore, or in ramshackle old houses crowded in dirty
towns. Soon he was called Brother Nicholas. Then, as time
went on, people called him Father Nicholas. Whenever he
appeared, they were glad to see him.

One summer day Father Nicholas walked along a leafy lane,
singing. He was happy because he had just found a good home
for two orphan children. He still had a long way to walk before
he would be back in Myra so he sat down to rest a bit and to
eat his lunch by a willow-fringed pool.

Just as he opened his sack and made ready to eat some bread
and cheese and dates and spicy cake, there came a sound. Was

it a child crying? He looked around and saw three children on the doorstep of a hut not far off. One of them was crying. When no one came to comfort the child, Nicholas picked up his lunch and hurried over to find out what was wrong.

Soon the children were telling him their troubles. Their mother and father had gone to work in the vineyards. There was nothing to eat in the house. They were all hungry. Nicholas dried their tears and spread his lunch before them. "See what I brought for you!" he exclaimed. In no time they were smiling, and he was waving good-by to them. He was hungry, but the children were happy. So he was happy, too.

Not a day passed when Nicholas did not make someone happy. And all the while he was taking more and more responsibility in the work of the church. However, one year he was able to take time to sail to the Holy Land, as he had been hoping to do for a long time.

One evening on a hilly pasture near the little town of Bethlehem, Nicholas stood with some shepherds watching the sheep. A lamb cuddled in his arms. All was still on the hillside and in the sleeping town. Was this such a night as that holy night when Christ was born? Nicholas looked at the starry heaven and thought of the angels' song of glory to God and peace on earth to men of good will.

The wonder of that song echoed in his heart during the voyage back to Myra. He wanted to share with everybody the joy and good will that Jesus brought to earth. He wrote to Anya and to the family of Thaddeus about Bethlehem and about watching the flocks by night in the fields. He promised to tell them more about the Holy Land when next he could go to

Patara. "However, it may not be for some time, for our good Bishop is very old and not well, and we all try to help him as much as we can," he wrote.

One evening, word came to him that the Bishop was dead. Very early the next morning Nicholas walked down to the Cathedral to pray. As he walked through the city, here and there small groups of Christians were gathered to talk about the good old Bishop and to wonder who the next Bishop would be. Nicholas wondered, too. He had no idea who would be chosen. But he prayed that he would be as good and kind a man as their old Bishop had been. Churchmen, he knew, would soon be meeting at the Cathedral to elect a new one.

As he came to the Cathedral, he realized that already the men were meeting. It seemed strange to him that he had not known about the meeting. He walked to the door of the church, and just then a churchman stepped forward. "Hail, Nicholas! You are to be Bishop of Myra!" the man said.

Nicholas was speechless. Surely he had heard wrong. Other churchmen gathered around, calling, "Hail, Nicholas, Bishop of Myra!" Nicholas was still too amazed to speak. He? A Bishop?

Boys passing by heard the men on the Cathedral steps proclaiming Nicholas Bishop. They ran down the street shouting, "Our friend, Good Father Nicholas, will be the new Bishop!" From place to place the word flew; and the Christians dropped their work and hurried to the Cathedral.

As the people came, Nicholas understood. He looked around at the churchmen and asked, "May I go inside alone to pray? I must ask God to help me do what is right."

Slowly he walked toward the front of the church, and, kneeling humbly, talked with God for a long while. He wanted to lead the people truly and be brave to do right no matter how great was the danger. He wanted to be a real follower of Jesus.

When he once more appeared at the Cathedral door, a crowd of people cheered. Children climbed nearby trees to see him better, and one little boy called down when the crowd was quiet for a moment, "Father Nicholas, we are happy that you will be Bishop. You are my friend."

"My friend, too," a little girl in the crowd sang out. She worked her way toward the front so as to be one of the first to follow the churchmen and the new Bishop into the Cathedral.

As Bishop, Nicholas was treated with great respect. A number of people called him Bishop Nicholas, which was

right. But he liked to be called Father Nicholas, and many spoke of him in that way; or they said "Good Father Nicholas," or sometimes just "Good Nicholas." Everyone knew it was he.

He had to travel to many churches and homes, so he bought a sleek white horse, swift and graceful——the kind of horse he had dreamed of owning when he was a boy. He named his horse North Star. As the North Star guided travelers by sea and land toward their homes, so the good Bishop's horse often brought him safely home through the dark after a long, weary day.

Bishop Nicholas and his horse were a welcome sight wherever they went. As they climbed the mountainsides to visit the shepherds, the shepherds' boys and girls ran across the grassy mountain pastures to meet him. Sometimes a father would tell the Bishop that his son was lazy and did not do his share of work. Then Good Nicholas would talk with the boy and point out what was right and wrong and urge him to do right.

When he rode down to the farms in the valleys, the farmers' children would see him and call, "Here comes Father Nicholas!" Then everyone would hurry to greet him and welcome him into their homes. If the children in a household had done wrong, Father Nicholas spoke with them kindly, but firmly. He loved children so much that he wanted them all to do their best. He was stern when it was for their own good; and they respected him and loved him very much.

Many a time he was in lonely, dangerous places. Late one afternoon he was riding down a mountain path when he saw a rough-looking man waving a sword and beckoning to others who lurked behind rocks a short distance away. Nicholas reined his horse up short. He knew at once that this was a wild robber band that had beaten farmers in the valley, stolen horses, and robbed a poor widow of silver coins she had hidden in a jar. Nicholas always carried a bag of gold coins, and no doubt they knew this. Were they waiting to beat him and rob him?

There was time to turn North Star around and escape into the hills before the robbers could follow. There Nicholas would be safe in the shepherds' encampment for the night. Knives glinted in the sun as the robbers crept behind the rocks nearer and nearer. Still Nicholas did not turn and gallop away. Instead he rode North Star right up to the robbers.

"Put those knives and swords on the ground," he called. "And your clubs, too. Now, all of you sit under that tree. I want to talk with you."

The robber chief was so astonished by Nicholas' courage that he dropped his knife. More knives, swords, and clubs clattered to the ground as Nicholas ordered, "Drop them all."

Then, while they gathered under the tree, he talked with them very seriously. Among other questions, he asked how they would like it if they were farmers, and robbers stole their horses. And did they not feel like cowards to steal a poor old woman's coins?

"Now," he said, "get the horses and lead them to their rightful owners. And take that silver to the widow's house."

He went with the robbers while they untied the stolen horses, hidden in an oak grove. The animals were frightened and ready to stampede, but he soothed them and coaxed them to start back to their homes. Stones rolled under the horses' hooves as the cavalcade moved downhill. Bishop Nicholas rode from one to another, patting the horses and talking with the men. He spoke so convincingly that two of the robbers decided to find honest work to do.

When news reached the valley that the robbers were coming back again, people fled into their houses and barred the doors. But one child, peeping through a partly open shutter cried, "Father Nicholas is leading the robber band." Then doors flew open, and people flocked out to welcome their brave Bishop.

Word of Bishop Nicholas' deed spread to the Christians through the valley, over the hills, and along the seashore. "A Bishop needs to be brave these days," some said; for they had heard about new persecutions of church leaders. Sailors brought word that the Emperor's soldiers were trying to stamp out all Christians. Many Bishops, and other Christians as well, had

68

been tortured and killed when they refused to give up being followers of Jesus.

Nicholas knew this. But he was determined to be brave for God. Meanwhile, from day to day, he kept on with his work.

9

Surprise Presents
for the Children

ONE DECEMBER afternoon Father Nicholas rode toward
Myra through a fishing village by the sea. The air was
unusually chill, and he looked forward to getting home. A warm
meal would taste good, and he would enjoy spending the evening quietly. Maybe he would write Anya a letter that Marcus
could take to her tomorrow when the donkey train came
through. How fortunate it was that Uncle John had taught
her to read and write.

Wind blew strong from Myra Bay. Nicholas pulled his cloak
about him and looked at the ships rocking at anchor. There
were more ships there for the winter than ever before. Astrono-
mers and wise men who studied the stars and the weather had
predicted a colder winter than was usual.

Suddenly someone called, "Father Nicholas, come. Please
help us." A girl of about eleven ran toward him from the

doorway of a hut. North Star stopped short. Nicholas listened while the girl explained that her mother was sick, the children were cold and hungry, and her father was far away.

Nicholas jumped from his horse, and North Star stood quietly while his master went into the hut with the girl.

The mother was coughing. The little ones were shivering.

"You shall have good food very soon," the good Bishop told them. He handed the older girl a coin. "Go to the inn and bring back a large bowl of stew and plenty of bread for all of you." She took the coin and ran off.

With the children clustering around him, he built up the fire and explained, "We will make a warm drink to soothe your mother's cough." He measured herbs from the little sack he always carried, and the children helped him stir the herbs in a cup of warm water.

They stood close while he helped their mother drink the healing medicine.

"You will feel much better soon," he promised her, "and the children will be frisky as little goats as soon as they have eaten a fine meal."

She smiled.

The smallest boy said, "I wish I had a toy goat."

"I'll tell you about some goats I knew when I was a boy," Father Nicholas said, sitting on a bench by the fire. The little girl climbed on his lap to hear the story. They liked it and wanted more stories.

"Do you know any stories about dolls?" she asked. "I lost my doll."

Just then the dinner arrived. The children swarmed around

the steaming bowl. Nicholas left quietly, and mounted North Star quickly. "We'll be back tonight," he told the horse as they rode away. North Star pricked up his ears and whinnied. They had been on many adventures together. He knew how to stand still and wait while his master left a present secretly and then how to gallop off quietly into the night.

Today he trotted briskly toward Myra while Father Nicholas whistled a merry tune. They stopped at a weaver's house. As Nicholas stepped inside, he was glad to see a pile of newly woven blankets. Amid the clatter and clack of the shuttle, the weaver did not notice his guest. But when he did see Father Nicholas, he left his loom at once and came forward.

"More blankets? So soon?" he asked, smiling.

"More blankets right now," Father Nicholas said, smiling, too. These two men shared a secret, although Father Nicholas never explained it fully. The first time he had come to the shop he had said to the weaver, "Will you please keep a stack of blankets on hand for me at all times? I will pay well for them; but please do not tell anyone in town how often I buy blankets from you."

At that time, too, the good bishop had asked the weaver's wife to make up cloaks and tunics for all sizes of children. "Just keep a stock of them on hand so I can get them whenever I need them. I will be very grateful to you if you will help me in this way," he had said. And he had given them several gold pieces in advance. Even if he had not paid so well, they would have been glad to help him; for they were Christians and liked to help the Bishop whenever they could. So the weaver's wife kept busy making clothing for children, even though in those days very little ready-made clothing was sold. Most of it was made at home.

When friends of the weaver's wife noticed that she had such a supply, they were surprised. "Who are these garments for?" they asked. "You have no children of your own who need clothes."

"Ssshhh! Do not spread the word around," she cautioned her friends. "Good Father Nicholas buys these. We do not know what children receive them; but you may be sure that they are happier because he is so kind."

"The old man who lives on the hillside path makes toys for Father Nicholas," the weaver further explained. "But this is all a secret," he added quickly, "so please don't talk about it to anyone."

This particular December evening the weaver could hardly wait to show Father Nicholas two new blankets. They were bright red, striped with soft green. "Just right for small children to snuggle in," he said.

"Just right!" Father Nicholas agreed, thinking of the two smallest children in the cottage by the sea. "And let me have that gold and blue blanket and this warm brown one, also."

As soon as he had selected enough blankets for all the family, Nicholas told the weaver to put them in a sack while he picked out clothes. The weaver called his wife; and when Nicholas went with her to the room where the garments were, the weaver quietly slipped one more blanket into the sack without charging for it.

It was dark by the time Nicholas and North Star reached the toymaker's house. The old man sat by the fire, making a

73

whipping-top. He arose and welcomed the Bishop gladly, and then went back to his work. He knew that Father Nicholas enjoyed looking around and picking out the special toys he wanted.

The first thing that went into the sack was a toy goat. Then a doll was laid in carefully. One toy followed another until the sack was full.

"We'll need another sack tonight," Father Nicholas said. "I am going to keep a stock of toys on hand at my house." A small room in the loft over North Star's stable was to be the toy room. The stable was one place where no one but Nicholas went. So no one but he and his horse would know where the toys were stored.

On reaching home, North Star rested in his stall and watched Father Nicholas light a lamp and place it in the doorway of the loft room. Then, guided by its glow, he lugged the sack of toys up the ladder. He had to laugh as he sorted them out on the floor. Green and yellow marbles rolled away and bumped a grumpy toy camel. What delightful toys that old man could make!

Nicholas put the playthings for the children he would visit that night in one sack. Then he arranged the other toys on the shelves—elephants, boats, tops, dolls, the grumpy camel beside a saucy donkey, and the many other things that he had so carefully selected.

As the last toy was put on the shelf, he heard someone calling him. It was one of the housekeeper's sons, sent to see if he was ready for supper. Quickly he blew out the light and tiptoed down the ladder.

"I shall come in shortly," he called.

Later that night, Nicholas loaded the sack of toys and other presents on North Star. Then he mounted and away they went, along the shore road toward the fishing village. The hut where the children lived stood alone and dreary at the edge of the village. Father Nicholas left North Star under a dark tree and tiptoed to the hut with the gifts. Carefully pushing the door open, he arranged the presents in a place where the children would see them in the morning and gently spread a new blanket over each sleeper.

' A child stirred in its sleep, but Nicholas was able to get away without being caught. North Star stepped proudly all the way home; and Nicholas chuckled with happiness as he thought of how surprised those children would be when they awoke. They were such pleasant, friendly children!

When Bishop Nicholas went to other countries on trips for the church, as he often did, children in those countries soon found out that he was their friend.

Once he helped some traveling school boys whom an innkeeper had treated cruelly and robbed. The good bishop found the boys and helped them return to their school safely. The tale of what he had done was told again and again, and added to by those who loved and admired the bishop.

Nicholas always enjoyed being with seamen and helping them, too. Once when he was on board ship during a raging storm, a seaman was knocked down and lay on deck nearly dead. Father Nicholas struggled through the wild wind, along the pitching deck. Any moment he could have been flung into the sea, but he went on until he reached the unconscious man. Risking his own life, Nicholas fought the storm and took the seaman to safety. Then, day and night, he patiently nursed the injured sailor back to health. Many travelers and seamen were astonished to see the sailor alive and well once more. "It's a miracle!" they cried. "Father Nicholas is a wonder worker!"

People enjoyed hearing these tales, and the stories spread far and wide. Soon he was so well known that people in many places feared for his safety, should persecution come again.

10

**Nicholas
and the Golden Gifts**

ALTHOUGH he made friends near and far, Father Nicholas
never forgot his old friends. One morning just as winter began, his ship made port in Myra. He was glad he had
reached home without having to winter-over in another harbor.
Many things were waiting for his attention, and there was
much to be done in the Cathedral. There was so much work
that months flew by before he had time to go to see his friends
in Patara.

Many years had passed since the day he had carried Anya's
belongings up to Thaddeus' house, yet he still remembered
how worried she had been about dowries for the girls. As he
thought about it one day, he realized with a start that Thekla
was more than old enough to marry. Is a marriage arranged
for her? he wondered.

He decided that he must soon go to Patara to find out how

77

the family was faring. Nicholas had not even seen Marcus the last few times the donkey' train had come through, because he had been busy in the Cathedral. Then, one windy March evening, the donkey train jingled to a stop at the gate. Marcus could not stay to visit, but he left a letter from Anya.

Alone in his study, Nicholas read it. Anya's writing was not good, but he could make out what she said. A wealthy young man from Greece wanted to marry Thekla. His ship had moored at Patara all winter, but he would leave soon. Thekla loved him, yet could not wed because she had no dowry. So the young man would have to sail away without her.

"Thekla talks of begging in the streets," Anya wrote, "to earn money to help her father and sisters."

Nicholas jumped up, knocking over the ink jar. He didn't even notice it. Thekla begging! Never! He hurried around, trying to make a plan while he tossed golden coins into a leather bag. "Thekla will have her dowry tonight," he murmured as he went to the stable where North Star slept.

North Star nuzzled Nicholas' neck and whinnied.

"Sssshh!" Nicholas patted the horse and led him quietly from the stable. "We mustn't make a sound when we reach Thaddeus' house," Nicholas whispered.

Before long they were passing through the sleeping city and onto the road toward Patara. Myriads of stars shone over shadowy villages, as North Star galloped on, mile after mile. While they dashed along the open road where the sea met sandy beaches, Nicholas sang. But when at last they reached Patara, they went quietly so as to awaken no one. A strong wind whistled from the bay; otherwise, all was still.

While they climbed the steep road toward Thaddeus' house, Nicholas wondered how he should leave the dowry so it would be found in the morning. The nearer he drew, the more puzzled he became. He could not leave his golden gift outside and run off. But he did not wish to be seen or heard.

North Star waited in the shadow of a tall pine tree while Nicholas tiptoed with his bag of gold toward the dark old house. One light flickered through a half-closed shutter. He edged closer. Inside the house he could see the nobleman, a sad, worried look on his face, wondering perhaps how he could get a dowry for Thekla.

Nicholas rushed forward, tripped over a stick, and bumped into a nut tree. He held his breath and stood in the shadows of the tree, motionless. Thaddeus had not heard. Nicholas then stepped quietly to

the window, slipped the sack into the room, and ran back to his horse.

Away he and North Star sped with the March wind; they passed through Patara before anyone awoke. As North Star galloped home, Nicholas laughed aloud, thinking of how surprised Thekla would be. How glad they would all be! Would Anya guess who had brought the gift?

Two weeks later the donkey train arrived once more in Myra from Patara. Marcus was bursting with good news. Not only did Father Nicholas and the family who kept house for him hear it, but Marcus talked so loud that passersby stopped at the Bishop's gate to listen and be glad. Marcus waved his arms in excitement as he talked. "Thekla has a dowry. Her father found a bag of gold in their house. Nobody knows who gave it. It's a mystery; but everybody is happy."

He was so carried away with Thekla's good fortune that he started off before he remembered to give Father Nicholas a letter from Thekla. He had to hurry back with it.

Everybody around wanted to hear what was in the letter, so Father Nicholas read parts of it out loud while the listeners smiled and nodded to each other. It bubbled with joy about the mysterious dowry and went on to explain that the wedding would be held the next month at her father's house. After that she and her husband would sail to his homeland. The letter ended: "Father Nicholas, nobody can guess who gave me the dowry. I keep thanking God for it, for I am sure he put it into someone's heart to be so kind. I am the happiest person. Please come to my wedding next month and give us your blessing."

So, one sunny spring day, Bishop Nicholas rode to Thekla's wedding. Along the Patara road he met a singing group of wedding guests dressed in their gayest clothes. They followed a farmer who played a long horn, while children decked with flowers danced beside them, clapping their hands.

So many people flocked to the wedding that a number of guests waited reverently outside the nobleman's house during the ceremony. When Father Nicholas and the bridal couple came out, he prayed for a blessing on everyone there. Then there was a great feast for everyone.

After Thekla sailed with her husband to her new home in the land of Greece, Bishop Nicholas saw Thaddeus' family quite often. Nicholas was now spending more time visiting the shepherd tribes in the mountain meadows beyond Patara. Sometimes, if Anya wanted to send him a message, she would give it to shepherd children who stopped at the house for a drink of water or some fruit before going farther up the mountain road.

When Nicholas visited Elena and Carita, they never tired of talking about their sister Thekla's dowry, and always said, "We wish we could find the person who gave it. We wish we could solve the mystery."

Nicholas just said "Umm!" and listened carefully for anything they might say that would show whether either of them hoped to marry soon.

The next summer Nicholas had to go on another sea voyage for the church. Before leaving he visited the shepherd tribes, comforting the sick, christening the babies, and telling the children Bible stories. Sometimes, if a family needed them, he left golden coins where the children would find them later.

The day before sailing, he was walking through a pasture a few miles beyond Patara with some shepherd children and their goats. One of the little girls said suddenly, "I'm sorry for the lady Elena. A young man from Italy wants to marry her. One day I saw them singing together to a bird perched high in a tree. Her father watched. He was sad. Anya says she cannot marry the young man because she has no dowry. Elena is very sad now."

Nicholas soon bade good-by to the children and rode down the mountain path, careful not to be seen. He rested by a pool near a waterfall until evening came. "North Star," he said, "it is well that we heard about Elena before I sailed; and fortunate there is enough gold for her dowry in the bag we have with us. They'll never guess who gave it. When it is found in the morning I shall be sailing out to sea."

When the purple evening shadows softly settled on the mountains, Nicholas rode nearer to Thaddeus' house. After dark he went to the window to which he had gone before, and again found it open. He left the dowry without a sound and sped off. Even after boarding his ship he still smiled to himself to think how surprised and glad Elena would be.

It was many months before he visited the big, old house once more. Then Carita limped to the door to greet him and poured out the delightful tale of Elena's wedding and of the mysterious dowry. She told him, "We could not even let you know about it because you were away. We cannot guess who left it. But we want to catch him and thank him."

"Indeed we do," her father agreed.

82

"I wonder if I shall ever have a dowry," Carita said wistfully. "But maybe nobody will want to marry me."

Thaddeus and Nicholas laughed; but Nicholas thought her father looked at her very thoughtfully. She was frail and shy and would need a very kind and strong husband.

Later, while riding to Myra, Nicholas thought how homesick Carita would be if she married and left her father and her old home. She loved Patara and its people. Often she invited children from the town to play in her father's meadows and orchards, and taught them games and happy songs. Everyone in Patara loved her.

That winter began with unusual cold and even snow. Bishop Nicholas and his helpers worked day and night to provide poor families with warm clothing, food, and fuel; for they were not ready for such weather. Whenever he went to buy warm things from the weaver and his wife, they always put something extra into the sack. Time and time again he bought toys from the old toymaker.

One December evening snow flurried over the Myra market place while Father Nicholas was buying baskets of bread for his helpers to take to the poor. Bells jingled. The donkey train from Patara trotted in. When Marcus, the driver, saw the Bishop, he sprang from his donkey and ran to tell his news.

"A very good man wants to marry the nobleman's daughter, Carita. He will repair her father's house and stock the pastures with flocks once more. All of Patara will benefit from such a marriage."

Marcus stopped short, somewhat abashed by the way he had blurted out his message to so important a person in a public place. He dug his toe in the snow, eager to tell the rest, but not knowing how.

Father Nicholas helped him out, patting his shoulder, and sharing a piece of bread with him. "I know, Marcus, you are worried because there is no dowry for Carita. And Anya is worried, too. But what can we do? No one seems to know who gave dowries to the other daughters."

Marcus busied himself with his donkeys as Nicholas mounted North Star slowly. He did not want to seem too eager to get away. He was just riding off when Marcus called, "I almost forgot. Anya told me to tell you that they have a new puppy. It barks at everyone who comes."

Umm! thought Nicholas. A barking puppy! It will be hard to leave a gift without being caught. But I must try.

Soon he had the bag of gold for Carita's dowry, and North Star was carrying him once more toward Patara. Roof tops lay white under snowy blankets. Snowflakes touched Father Nicholas' beard with white. The horse's hooves scarcely sounded on the snowy road that stretched for mile after mile.

As North Star climbed the hill toward Thaddeus' house, Nicholas thought of the first Christmas. Maybe on such a night as this shepherds watching their flocks near Bethlehem heard the song of peace and good will and went to find the baby in the manger. Maybe on a night like this the three kings rode from the East with gifts of gold and frankincense and myrrh.

On reaching the pine tree where he had waited before, North Star stopped. Nicholas dismounted, pulled up his furry collar, and stepped cautiously toward the house carrying the

bag of gold. How slippery the snow was! His boots crunched through it. Everyone must be sleeping, even the puppy. Once again the shutter was open; but this time not quite enough. And it seemed to be stuck. Nicholas tugged on it to open it more. It creaked as it finally gave way, and Nicholas dropped the gold, clinking, to the floor.

Bow-wow! Bow-wow-wow! The puppy rushed to the window, barking. Nicholas dashed away, slipped, and plunged into a snowdrift. While he struggled to get out, people hurried through the house with lighted candles. He heard the shout, "Here's another dowry!"

The front door burst open. Somebody cried, "There he is in the snowdrift. Catch him!"

A tall young man ran out and pulled Nicholas from the drift. Nicholas tried hard to get away. But his boots were slippery, and the young man pulled him steadily toward the house. The yapping puppy slid down the steps, grabbed Nicholas' cloak, and tugged him along. Thaddeus hurried out and caught Nicholas' hand and drew him on. Everyone was laughing and exclaiming, "We've caught him, whoever he is."

Suddenly the moon flooded the hill with silver light. Nicholas tried to pull down his furry cap closer over his face so they wouldn't see it. But Anya came out, too, and clung to his cloak to pull him up the steps.

In the doorway, Carita held a candle. When it shone on Nicholas' face, they all cried, "It's Good Father Nicholas."

"God bless you good Nicholas, servant of God," said Thaddeus. "How can we ever thank you?"

"Do not thank me," Nicholas answered, as soon as he could

get his breath. "If good fortune comes your way, thank God."

The young man who had caught Nicholas led him to a chair inside. "You must be cold and tired," he said as he shook snow from Nicholas' cloak.

Nicholas liked him, especially when he promised, "I shall do my best to make Carita happy. I would have married her without a dowry if I could have, but both her father and my father forbade it."

Carita's father, happier than Nicholas could ever remember, thanked him again.

"The way you can thank me," Nicholas said to Thaddeus, "is to promise not to tell who left the golden gifts."

But Thaddeus would make no such promise. Instead he said, "Maybe sometimes I shall hide gifts for the shepherds' children and let them think Father Nicholas brought them."

"I shall help you!" Carita's future husband exclaimed. "I will leave the presents for them at night and run away."

Carita's eyes sparkled with an exciting idea and she clapped her hands, saying, "After I am married, I shall bake sweet cakes often for poor children and pretend Father Nicholas sent them."

"I'll help you," Anya said. "And when we write your sisters about your dowry, we will tell them how we plan to help Good Nicholas give surprises to children. Perhaps they will want to do the same."

11
Bishop Nicholas,
Brave Prisoner

SHORTLY AFTER SUNRISE the next morning, Anya hurried down the road to the Patara market place to tell about the dowries. The day had turned suddenly warm, and the snow was melting fast. In the golden sunshine by the fruit vendor's stall, people collected around her, laughing and chattering about the good news.

From village to village and on to Myra the story spread. One little boy there said to his mother, "Perhaps Good Nicholas left that golden coin we found in my shoe last month." Everyone began to tell of mysterious gifts they thought Father Nicholas had given.

Before long, for miles around people caught the spirit of giving without telling. Their hearts were light whenever they left a sack of toys or food or clothing and hurried away without being seen or thanked. In time, whenever a mysterious gift was found, children would say, "Good Nicholas has been here."

Other people went quietly to the Bishop to ask the names of children who needed special things. "We'll be glad to help you any time," they said.

Then one day, Marcus rushed to Bishop Nicholas' door, white with terror. "Fly for your life," he cried. "The Emperor's soldiers are coming to destroy Christian churches and scriptures and arrest Christian leaders."

Bishop Nicholas shook his head. "My true friend, Marcus, do not be afraid for me. If the soldiers arrest me, they will spare my people. Hurry to other towns and warn Christians. Advise them to hide the scripture. Urge them to be brave for God, and to believe that what is right can never be destroyed by cruel might. Remind them that God is stronger than any ruler on earth. Hurry, Marcus. You are God's messenger today!"

As Marcus left, Bishop Nicholas hailed some boys who were playing in the streets. "Run through the town and call people to come to the Cathedral," he called. The boys dashed off shouting while the Bishop walked swiftly to the church. Quickly he gathered the scriptures and ran with them toward the stable. They were the very writings that Uncle John had copied years before.

Swiftly, Father Nicholas climbed to the room above North Star's stall and made straight for a place he had prepared for a time such as this. He wrapped the scriptures in a soft goat skin and slid them in a secret place. Then he pulled a toy chest in front and set as guards on it a saucy wooden donkey, some sheep, and a camel caravan. Nobody would suspect that the room held anything but toys.

Nicholas hurried down the ladder, gave North Star one last pat, and returned to the Cathedral. People were running toward it, shouting, "What is wrong?" By the time he reached the reading desk, a large crowd of people had come in answer to his request.

Nicholas raised his hand as if in blessing, and all was suddenly silent. He wasted no time as he explained that soldiers were coming to arrest him.

Someone cried, "Escape! Escape Father Nicholas! We'll help you!"

But he answered, "If I run away, they might burn your homes and torture your children to try to force you to tell where I am. If I am arrested, do not try to stop the soldiers, but let me go quietly. Be brave; trust God. Promise me you will be kind to each other and share what you have with the poor, and be especially good to children."

With one voice they answered, "We promise."

A bugle shattered the air. Soldiers marched in. They carried a statue of the emperor. Some persons screamed; but Nicholas raised his hand to remind them to keep quiet and remain in their places.

The captain, a huge man with a gleaming helmet, brandished his sword and ordered Nicholas to worship the statue of the emperor and to surrender the sacred scriptures that they might be burned.

A great hush fell upon the people as Nicholas walked calmly from the reading desk toward the captain.

"I will not bow to the emperor as to a god. I will not give you our scriptures to be burned. I confess before the world that I believe in one God, the Father of all people, and that I am a loyal follower of Jesus Christ." He told the captain that he would submit to arrest if the captain would promise that the soldiers would not harm the people.

Some people wept. Some fainted. But all remained in their places. The captain sent soldiers to search the Cathedral and the Bishop's house for the scriptures, and ordered others to bind the Bishop's arms to his sides with a rope. Surrounded by soldiers, Nicholas was led from the Cathedral.

Tears blurred his eyes as he left, yet he called to the people, "Trust God; and follow Jesus' example." As the soldiers took him down to a wharf, the searchers returned and reported to the captain. "We have

looked everywhere but find no sign of the books. We even went in the loft of the stable but found only toys."

The captain said to Nicholas; "I will ask the judge not to have you killed if you tell us where the scriptures are."

But Nicholas stood firm. "I will not tell."

They hurried him along the wharf and took him aboard a ship. Without another word, the soldiers threw him into a dark, narrow cell in the filthy hold.

Never leaving that cell for weeks, Nicholas was tossed back and forth while the ship wallowed through one storm after another at sea. He ached all over because there was no room to lie down and rest. His lips and throat were parched with thirst. Hunger gnawed at him day after day. A few sips of water and a crust of bread were all he had each day to eat and drink.

In spite of his own suffering, he prayed for his people often and for all who were persecuted because of their faith in God. Three times a soldier appeared at the cell door and told him that if he would deny his religion, worship the emperor, and turn over the sacred writings he could go free. But Nicholas was loyal to God.

After what seemed months he was hauled from the ship and marched up a stony path to a judgment hall. Weak with hunger and stiff from his cramped cell, he could barely hobble. Yet he did not fall by the wayside. The cold-eyed judges gave him one more chance to worship the emperor.

Nicholas wanted to be free. He wanted to go home and be with his friends. But he could not accept freedom and comfort if it meant turning away from God. So he looked straight at the judges and bravely confessed his obedience to God as a loyal follower of Jesus.

Hard hands dragged him over rough, cold, stone steps down to a muddy cell in the dungeon. This cell was even narrower than the one on shipboard. When Nicholas tried to sleep, he hunched up on the floor with his back against the chill stone wall. Day dragged into night, and night into day. Day after day and night after night went by. He lost track of time and could not tell whether he had been there several months or several years.

The jailers never spoke to him, but just thrust in a bit of food once a day. When he tried to tell them about their kind Father God, someone farther off, the head jailor perhaps, ordered them away. This voice in the distance was the only voice besides his own that he ever heard.

One morning he sat in his cell thinking about home. How were the people of Myra? Would anyone let them know when he was killed? If one of his friends should see him before he died, would he be recognized? In the semi-darkness he could see that his beard had grown white; but he knew he had not been in prison long enough for this to happen naturally. Could it be from hunger and thirst and loneliness and sorrow? Such things, he reasoned, could turn hair white.

Suddenly soldiers clattered down the stairs shouting, "Release the prisoner! The new emperor says Christian prisoners are to go free!"

Nicholas could hardly believe his ears. A great hope welled up in his heart as he dragged himself to his feet. If it were only true!

93

A burly jailer hurried to his cell saying, "A boat is ready to sail for Myra. You must board it quickly." The key rasped in the lock, and the jailer pulled Nicholas from the cell. "You're free now."

Free? As suddenly as that? Trembling with joy, Nicholas stood and thanked God. The jailer hustled him along, "You must leave here quickly. You should have been released months ago."

Two soldiers pushed Nicholas up the stairs and out into the dawn, all talking excitedly together. The captain of the guard had made a mistake in reading an order from the emperor some months before. Now everyone at the prison wanted to get Bishop Nicholas back to Myra before the governor learned of the mistake.

Although he was terribly stiff from his imprisonment, the joy of going home sped his steps. The fresh air smelled better than he ever remembered. Spring flowers nodded in the early morning breeze along the road to the wharf.

"Where am I?" Nicholas asked, "Is this one of the coastal islands off my homeland?"

The biggest soldier answered, "We cannot tell you. The captain wants no trouble."

Nicholas did not really care where he was. He wanted only to forget the months of sorrow and be happy in every day that lay ahead.

In a short time Nicholas was aboard a ship, and the ship was under way. He let the sea breeze fill his lungs and revive him. What joy to behold the sky again; to see the sun in all its beauty and feel its warmth!

94

He stretched his aching arms as wide as he could. How good to move without bumping a cold, stone wall!

A sailor smiled and said, "Good morning, Father Nicholas. May I help you?"

It was hard to walk after the long time in the narrow, damp cell. Nicholas gladly accepted the help the sailor offered. He walked on deck; but he tired so quickly that before long he had to lie down on the comfortable bed provided for him. He sank onto it gratefully and fell asleep. As the days on board ship passed, the sleep and the good food slowly made him stronger.

Then one day as he raised himself from a nap, there was a bustle of activity on board. When Nicholas looked up, he realized that they were in Myra Harbor! Dozens of rowboats were pulling through the waters and people were shouting, "Is Father Nicholas on your ship?"

The sailors sang out proudly, "Yes, we are bringing Father Nicholas home."

At the wharf were many people, dancing and singing and shouting their greetings. Even North Star was there, prancing and whinnying with the excitement.

Older boys gently lifted their Bishop onto North Star and walked beside him into the city. People lined the roads waving blossoms and calling a welcome. And all the way children sang and strewed flowers before him.

12

Good Nicholas' Helpers

I T WAS A LONG WHILE before Bishop Nicholas was strong enough to do many of the things he had done before his imprisonment. But the first thing he did do was bring the scripture from its hiding place. Some of the younger children had never heard readings from the sacred works. Their older brothers and sisters remembered a little, and they liked hearing the wonderful stories once again. And all of the adults were anxious to hear the teachings once more. . .

Whatever Bishop Nicholas read from the scriptures, he explained so that all could understand. He talked with his people so they realized that God is the father of all people everywhere. Father Nicholas had traveled so much that he could describe people who lived in Asia, in Africa, and in Europe. He pointed out how wonderful it was that so many of them heard the same words and tried in the same way to be good Christians.

"Not only do you who live in Myra," explained the Bishop, "know that Jesus said we must love God and obey him and love other people and treat them kindly; but people in many, many lands know these teachings, also."

One day some of the older boys and girls came to him with a special idea. When they were little, sometimes he had given them surprises. Now they wanted to help him surprise other children, smaller than themselves.

Father Nicholas beamed with pleasure. He beckoned them to crowd around his chair so that a group of little children playing under a nearby fig tree would not hear. The boys and girls came close, and he whispered what they could do.

Soon they were quietly running up and down the ladder from the toy room, bringing toys to a room in the house. Some of the boys set up a workbench. The girls mixed paints and dressed dolls. The boys made new toys and repaired old ones. Day after day, when they had time, Father Nicholas' helpers worked in the toy shop.

Then often at night someone filled a sack with toys and went secretly to the home of a poor family, silently leaving the gifts and disappearing mysteriously. The next day Father Nicholas and his helpers would laugh together to think how happy the children were because of the mysterious presents.

As he grew to be an old man, Nicholas became more feeble. Nevertheless, he was always kind and friendly, and his eyes always twinkled merrily when someone told about leaving presents for children and not being caught.

One day when some people came to see him, he looked so frail and ill that they were greatly disturbed. As they were

leaving, they said to each other, not thinking he heard, "What shall we do when good Father Nicholas dies?"

He heard them and said, "Do not be sad because I may leave you soon. Remember to follow Jesus; be kind to each other, generous to the poor, and give happiness to children. You must realize, too, that when I die I shall go home to heaven and a wonderful new life with God."

Somehow, they understood; and it was not long before his words came true. One clear, beautiful morning on the sixth of December, the news was spread that Nicholas, the brave and kind Bishop of Myra, had gone to his wonderful new life. His people gathered on their doorsteps and in the market place and then walked in groups to the cathedral, talking about how much they would miss him.

One said, "This is Father Nicholas' birthday in heaven. We must always remember it in a very special way, a way that would make him glad."

Some children ran by. On seeing them, one man said softly, "Father Nicholas always tried to be like Jesus. Jesus was a friend to children, and so was he. Let us be his helpers and do happy things for them. On this day especially, let us give presents to the little ones and pretend he sent the gifts."

So it was that little children continued to receive presents at night in a mysterious way from Good Father Nicholas. The pleasant custom of giving without telling or waiting to be thanked spread to many other lands—to wherever children are loved.

In time Nicholas became known as St. Nicholas, and tales about his kindness to children spread far and wide. Since people everywhere love children and like to make them happy, each year more and more people shared the glad secret about St. Nicholas and joined the merry band of his mysterious helpers.

BOOK II
HOW THE SAINT NICHOLAS LEGEND SPREAD

1

Stories, Songs and Pictures
about Saint Nicholas

NOT MANY YEARS after Bishop Nicholas died, he was called St. Nicholas in various countries. Groups of people in different places chose him for their special protector, their patron saint. The Feast of St. Nicholas, December 6, became a special holiday. Naturally, his name was pronounced somewhat differently in different languages (as, for instance, Charles is Carl, Carlos, etc.); but no matter how people spoke his name, they loved St. Nicholas.

Nobody knows exactly when all the various people chose St. Nicholas for a patron saint, nor just how some stories about him began and grew and spread and became legends. Travelers journeying over deserts and mountains by camel caravans and donkey trains told tales of the friendly saint. Foot travelers, resting by village wells in green and sheltered valleys, told stories about him to villagers who came to draw water. Sailors sang of him and recounted legends of the wonders that he worked.

When a new church was built in Myra, it was named the Church of St. Nicholas. Through the years, hundreds of churches in many different seaports were named for him; for he became the sailors' patron saint.

One St. Nicholas church was built during the 11th century in Bari, in southern Italy, on a peninsula extending into the Adriatic Sea. It faces the Near East where Nicholas was born. This Church of San Nicole is famous for its silver altar and silver ceiling. Thousands of people go there each year for the San Nicole festival, held by sailors and fishermen. Children sing about him in the streets as his statue is brought from the church and carried a short way out to sea. People strew flowers along the road and on the waters as the statue passes by; and at evening they welcome it back with bonfires, torches, and fireworks.

When he became the children's patron saint in Greece, girls and boys danced in his honor on the hillsides and along the shores of the sea. In Greek his name means "conqueror of the people," and many agree that he conquered with his kindness.

More than six hundred years after Nicholas lived in Patara, a Russian ruler, called Vladimir the Great, married a princess from Constantinople. He became a Christian and built Christian schools in Russia. Then the Russian children heard stories about St. Nicholas, and they were happy to have him for patron saint. Sometimes they found cakes on their window sills; and their parents said, "St. Nicholas left those cakes. You know he always shared his food with other people."

Children everywhere enjoyed sitting by the fire on a cold night and hearing about the wonderful things St. Nicholas did.

Legends about him spread to Lapland, where reindeer roam the snowy tundras, forests, and plains. Lapp children were enchanted when a traveler who sought shelter for the night from the icy winds could tell tales of the kind old saint who brought presents to children. Naturally, they thought he rode on a sleigh drawn by reindeer, because that was how people traveled in their part of the world.

St. Nicholas became very popular in England, too, and in time more than 400 churches were named for him. Even today, in some country places in Northern England, when a fine girl who is poor wishes to marry, some kind neighbors give her mysterious presents at night, as Nicholas did for the daughters of the nobleman of Patara.

About seven hundred years ago when many of the famous Cathedrals in Europe were being built, legends about St. Nicholas became connected with some. At that time a most beautiful

Cathedral was erected at Chartres in Northern France; and many French people gladly worked on the building. Some even harnessed themselves to carts and pulled the gray stone from the quarry for the walls. Sculptors and artists told stories in paintings and stained glass—the most exquisite stained glass ever seen.

On the dedication day (1260) people thronged the roads to Chartres. Inside the Cathedral they saw windows that told of St. Nicholas and the three maidens of Patara. As they gazed in wonder, the windows with their marvelous blue glass sections shone like jewels in the sunlight. The saint and the three girls almost seemed alive. Those who stood admiring the windows caught the glad spirit of giving that spread wherever tales of St. Nicholas were told.

On St. Nicholas' Eve in many European countries parents helped children set out wooden or leather shoes. While the children slept, the grown people had a good time putting candies, nuts, fruits, and other little gifts into the shoes.

Some people think the custom of hanging up stockings to receive presents began in Italy; others say in Germany, or France. Some say that when St. Nicholas threw a dowry through the window it caught in a stocking drying by the fire, and that's how the custom of hanging up stockings began.

Anyway, small Italian and French girls who boarded at convent schools often hung up their stockings. On St. Nicholas Eve, each girl wrote the saint a letter saying she had been good during the year and asking for some special present. Then, while older girls lighted the way with candles, the younger ones hurried down the hall and placed the stockings with notes on them at the door of the abbess in charge of the school. Back to bed they ran, pulled up the covers, and dreamed of St. Nicholas.

Sometimes, a little girl would lie awake wondering about St. Nicholas. Then suddenly a ray of light would come through the dark as the abbess' door was opened. And the abbess, some of the sisters, and the older girls, would fill the stockings. Whispering and laughing softly, they were enjoying being St. Nicholas' helpers. The little girl watching understood right then the wonderful secret of St. Nicholas. Knowing the secret made it better than ever! Next year she would be a helper!

School children had fun acting in St. Nicholas plays, too. Crowds always came when the play called "The Three Daughters" was given at the gateway of an abbey. The watchers were breathless when St. Nicholas tiptoed to the house, threw in a dowry, and dashed off without being seen. Everyone cheered and clapped when he was caught after giving the third dowry!

In many places, Christmas preparations began right after St. Nicholas Eve, December 5. The few weeks before Christmas are called the Advent season. During these days people prepare for Jesus' birthday with praying, special music and carols, and church services. St. Nicholas has long been considered a messenger to help children make their hearts ready to receive the Christ Child.

Adults everywhere have dressed as St. Nicholas dressed and have visited children on St. Nicholas' Eve. In times past, as today, in many villages in Europe, the children wait on the 5th of December for the saint. While waiting, they sing songs that tell how good he was. And finally, the village schoolmaster, or some other adult who knows the children well, comes in a red robe trimmed with white fur and a tall, ornamented cap, called a Bishop's miter. Sometimes he is mounted on a white horse and he always carries a sack of sweets and other small presents.

The children hurry to greet him as he comes to the door. First he talks with them, and then he opens his sack and strews out the good things he has brought for the children.

In some places he talks with the children and finds out what they hope the Christ Child will give them for Christmas. Then, during the night, he leaves small gifts in their shoes or stockings. And on Christmas Eve or Christmas Day the children receive bigger presents which they think the Christ Child (or Christ Kind) has given them.

2

The Wonderful Legend
Comes to America

SEVERAL hundred years ago, many children and their families were making a long journey to a new land. They were coming to America to live and make their homes. Among the first people who came were the Dutch, who built homes in the area we call New York, but which they called New Amsterdam.

The Dutch children brought with them many of their customs and holidays, and among them was St. Nicholas Day, or Sinterklaas Day as many called it. Some called him "San Nicolaas," or "San Claus," or "Sint-Niklaas." His holiday was the gayest of the whole year in old New Amsterdam. He was the favorite saint of the city, and the first Dutch church in America was named for him. Some people say that his statue was the figurehead on the ship that brought the Dutch here.

When December winds whistled across New Amsterdam

harbor and rattled the doors of the gay-colored little houses, the Dutch children helped their mothers make Sinterklaas cakes. And on St. Nicholas Eve he would come, just as he had in Holland, bringing them gifts and candy. Good children put oats and carrots in their shoes for his horse.

Everyone loved the happy excitement of St. Nicholas Day in New Amsterdam; and naturally, after some years, when English children arrived, they, too, wanted to share in the good time and the gifts. Since they did not wear wooden shoes, their parents suggested they hang their stockings by the fireplace.

In the New World, as he had done in the Old World, St. Nicholas came in different ways. Germans in Pennsylvania farmlands called him Pelznickel ("Nicholas dressed in fur"), and he blustered into their farmhouses on a wintry evening.

As people came from many countries, they brought to the United States a great variety of holiday customs. In time these customs mingled together. Whereas children from many places received small gifts on St. Nicholas Eve, some also received bigger surprise presents on Christmas; some, on New Year; and others, on January 6 which they called Epiphany or Three Kings Day. In time a number of people agreed that Jesus' birthday was the perfect day for presents; although, of course, the pleasant custom of receiving small gifts on St. Nicholas' Eve was also continued by many.

At first, Puritan children in New England did not celebrate Christmas with music and excitement and gifts. But on Christmas Day they shared with the poor. After a while, though, New England joined the whole country in celebrating Christmas as the most heart-warming time of year.

3

Here Comes Santa Claus

L EGENDS about St. Nicholas were not the only tales about
December holidays that came from everywhere to
America. There were many stories about a kind old man who
gave surprise presents to children. Some called him Father
Christmas, or the Christmas Man, or the Yule Man or
Bonhomme Noel, or other names.

During December people in cold countries have always built
cheery fires on their hearths and gathered around to enjoy the
warmth and friendliness. Centuries ago, people in Germany
and various parts of northern Europe used to think a good-
natured, blustering old man rode down from the North through
the air in a chariot, fighting the giants of ice and snow with the
warmth of fire. They called him the god Thor and believed
that (although they could not see him) he came down their
chimneys into their home fires, making everyone cheerful and

friendly. If people had quarreled, they were expected to make up and become friends again by their warm December firesides.

Some thought, too, that another good spirit of the home (Hertha) gently drifted down to·their hearths on the smoke of their fir and pine branch fires.

So, out of many old, old tales from the Old World, came a new, jolly fairy-tale person as part of the Christmas celebration in the New World. This new pretend person was called Santa Claus, which, of course, was one of St. Nicholas' names. Since St. Nicholas had shown how to give presents without telling, especially to children, Santa Claus began to do the same; and, copying St. Nicholas legends, people caught the spirit of giving secretly and began acting the part of Santa Claus.

Even though Santa Claus is not really St. Nicholas, but a gay Christmas symbol of the way St. Nicholas gave, children often spoke of him as St. Nicholas. Of course, they wondered how he looked and traveled. At first some children thought he rode a white pony. Many Dutch children in America said he rode over roof tops in a wagon drawn by horses. Probably children from Scandinavia and nearby snowy regions said he came by reindeer sleigh; and they may have thought, too, he came by way of the North Pole.

Two little girls in New York were talking about such things one morning before Christmas more than a hundred years ago. "Let's ask Father," the taller one suggested. So they ran down to breakfast calling, "Good morning, Father. Please tell us what St. Nicholas looks like and how he comes to us."

Their father, Dr. Clement Moore, smiled. He had often seen pictures of the brave, kind Bishop Nicholas; but he realized the girls wanted to know about the make-believe Santa Claus.

As Dr. Moore stirred his coffee, his eyes twinkled. He had an idea! "On Christmas Eve, I'll tell you how he looks," he promised. A verse already was beginning to run through his mind.

However, not until Christmas Eve as he drove home through the snowy streets with presents for his children hidden in the sleigh, did Dr. Moore really know just how the poem should go. People passed in the frosty evening calling "Merry Christmas" to one another. Children in some houses were already hanging stockings by the fire. All of this helped him as he drove on, making up his verse to the tune of the sleighbells.

When he reached home, he hurried to the library to write his poem down, calling to his children, "After supper, I'll have something to read you."

As soon as supper was over, the girls hung up their stockings. Then they curled in chairs by the fire, ready to listen. Their father began,

"'Twas the night before Christmas, when all through the
    house
Not a creature was stirring, not even a mouse."
The girls were delighted and listened to every word that fol-lowed. They giggled and nodded about:

" . . . a miniature sleigh with eight tiny reindeer
With a little old driver so lively and quick,
I knew in a moment it must be St. Nick."

When their father finished, they danced around and clapped their hands. What fun that story was!

Although Dr. Moore thought little more about it, a friend

had the poem printed the next Christmas Eve (1823) in a newspaper in Troy, New York, under the title, "A Visit from St. Nicholas." Before long it began to be printed in children's books and illustrated with pictures.

One day, about forty years later, some children saw a picture drawn by a man named Thomas Nast. In the picture, Santa Claus sat on a box marked "North Pole," smiling as children came to see him from all over the world. Immediately, children who saw it said, "Santa Claus' workshop is at the North Pole. That's where he keeps his reindeer and sleigh." They began addressing letters to him at the North Pole, as boys and girls still do today.

All through Advent season, children everywhere make ready for the mysterious beauty of Christmas Eve. On that evening candles glow in windows all over the world to welcome the Christ Child on his birthday. Then children everywhere—in busy seaports or quiet mountain villages, in big houses or tiny cottages—listen gladly to the story of the baby in the manger and the angels' songs of peace and good will. They gaze at the stars in the Christmas sky and think of the wise men who followed a star to Jesus.

Then they hang up their stockings or set out their shoes and jump into bed, to dream of what Santa Claus will bring. And Santa Claus comes in the form of someone who loves children and gives without telling, just as Saint Nicholas gave long ago.

Story of St. Nicholas

Boston Public Library

ORIENT HEIGHTS
BRANCH LIBRARY

18 Barnes Avenue
East Boston 28

The Date Due Card in the pocket indicates the date on or before which this book should be returned to the Library.

Please do not remove cards from this pocket.

(Continued from front flap)

Mildred C. Luckhardt has long been interested in the legends of Saint Nicholas and Santa Claus. But her story is not just a retelling of old legends. Instead, she has read widely to find out how people lived and what the Christian church was like in the days when Nicholas rode about on his horse, North Star.

As a result, her story of the good saint, although based on legend, tells what really might have happened. The last section of the book tells how the legends about him grew, and how our Santa Claus came to be.

Mildred C. Luckhardt was born in New York City, but now resides in Rye, New York.

She studied Christian Education at Teacher's College, Columbia, and for seven years was Director of Christian Education at Rye Presbyterian Church. She now lectures to various denominations on the Bible and Christian Education. In addition to numerous books, she has also written many articles, song lyrics, plays, and devotional stories.

ABINGDON PRESS
New York   Nashville

CPSIA information can be obtained
at www.ICGtesting.com
Printed in the USA
LVHW080920101221
705842LV00011B/644